Most everyone believes charity is essential to social improvement. But most everyone also has a limited – and many have a false – understanding of what charity is, and what it can or should do. This is why books like this one are so valuable to help us better understand the underlying logic, tremendous benefits – and yes, the real limitations – of charity.

– Michael Moody, Grand Valley State University, USA

DOI: 10.1057/9781137522658.0001

Also by John Mohan

DON'T LOOK BACK? Voluntary and Charitable Finance of Hospitals in Britain, Past and Present *(with M. Gorsky)*

MUTUALISM AND HEALTH CARE: British Hospital Contributory Schemes in the 20th Century *(with M. Gorsky, T. Willis)*

Also by Beth Breeze

HOW DONORS CHOOSE CHARITIES

RICHER LIVES: Why Rich People Give *(with Theresa Lloyd)*

THE READER ON PHILANTHROPY *(co-edited with Michael Moody)*

DOI: 10.1057/9781137522658.0001

palgrave▶pivot

The Logic of Charity: Great Expectations in Hard Times

John Mohan

Director, Third Sector Research Centre,
University of Birmingham, UK

and

Beth Breeze

Director, Centre for Philanthropy,
University of Kent, UK

palgrave
macmillan

DOI: 10.1057/9781137522658.0001

First published 2016 by
PALGRAVE MACMILLAN

The authors have asserted their rights to be identified as the authors of this work in accordance with the Copyright, Designs and Patents Act 1988.

Palgrave Macmillan in the UK is an imprint of Macmillan Publishers Limited, registered in England, company number 785998, of Houndmills, Basingstoke, Hampshire, RG21 6XS.

Palgrave Macmillan in the US is a division of Nature America, Inc., One New York Plaza, Suite 4500 New York, NY 10004–1562.

Palgrave Macmillan is the global academic imprint of the above companies and has companies and representatives throughout the world.

Hardback ISBN: 978–1–137–52263–4
E-PUB ISBN: 978–1–137–52264–1
E-PDF ISBN: 978–1–137–52265–8
DOI: 10.1057/9781137522658

Distribution in the UK, Europe and the rest of the world is by Palgrave Macmillan*, a division of Macmillan Publishers Limited, registered in England, company number 785998, of Houndmills, Basingstoke, Hampshire RG21 6XS.

Library of Congress Cataloging-in-Publication Data is available from the Library of Congress.

A catalog record for this book is available from the Library of Congress.

A catalogue record for the book is available from the British Library.

To our families:
Ellie, Jenny and Clare;
Michael, Beren and Meredith

DOI: 10.1057/9781137522658.0001

Contents

DOI: 10.1057/9781137522658.0001

List of Illustrations

Figures

▶

Tables

DOI: 10.1057/9781137522658.0002

Acknowledgements

Personal acknowledgements

With sincere thanks to all the charity leaders, staff, volunteers, donors, philanthropy advisers, corporate philanthropy managers, giving circle hosts and members and everyone else who participated in the research presented in this book. Without your willingness to share information and to reflect on your experiences, we would be less able to understand the logic of charity.

Formal acknowledgements

The funding by the Economic and Social Research Council (ESRC) and the partner funders of the Centre for Charitable Giving and Philanthropy (CGAP)is gratefully acknowledged (ESRC ref: RES-593–25–0003).

With thanks to academic colleagues who were partners in some of the research presented in this book: Peter Backus, David Clifford, Angie Eikenberry, Eddy Hogg, Rose Lindsey and Theresa Lloyd.

We are also grateful to colleagues at the Charities Aid Foundation (CAF) and at the Association of Chief Executives of Voluntary Organizations (ACEVO), who helped to recruit samples for the research discussed in Chapters 4 and 5. David Clifford and Peter Smith of the University of Southampton designed the sample of the accounts of 10,000 registered charities which forms the basis of the data presented in Chapter 2. The Centre for Data Digitisation and Analysis

(CDDA), Queen's University, Belfast, carried out the extraction of the data. David Kane and Pete Bass (National Council for Voluntary Organizations – NCVO) devised and implemented procedures for classifying the financial information from those accounts. We also acknowledge the team behind the British Social Attitudes survey at NatCen, whose questions on charitable giving from the 1991 survey we repeated in our updated data on public attitudes, presented in Chapter 1.

With thanks to Pears Foundation, who funded the research on '*Richer Lives: Why Rich People Give*', discussed in Chapters 4 and 5.

We are greatly indebted to all the above although we alone are responsible for the analyses and commentary presented here.

DOI: 10.1057/9781137522658.0003

List of Abbreviations

AOB	Area of Benefit
AOO	Area of Operation
ACEVO	Association of Chief Executives of Voluntary Organizations
BSA	British Social Attitudes
CAF	Charities Aid Foundation
CSJ	Centre for Social Justice
ICNPO	International Classification of Nonprofit Organizations
IMD	Index of Multiple Deprivation
LA	Local Authority
NAVCA	National Association for Voluntary and Community Action
NCVO	National Council for Voluntary Organizations
NSTSO	National Survey of Third Sector Organizations
SIB	Social Impact Bond
SORP	Statement of Recommended Practice

palgrave▶**pivot**

www.palgrave.com/pivot

1

Introduction: Is There a 'Logic of Charity'?

Abstract: *Despite charity being a consistent feature of life in the UK, we lack a clear understanding of what charity is, how it operates, who it benefits and what it can and cannot be expected to do. We begin by summarizing the different organizing principles found in government and charity, and note that the logic guiding charitable activity is not well understood by politicians who seek to encourage charity and harness it in support of their political programmes. The historic role and contemporary nature of charity are reviewed, then a discussion of data on public attitudes regarding the role that charity does and should play in relation to government funding highlights how those attitudes have endured and changed over the past 25 years.*

Mohan, John and Beth Breeze. *The Logic of Charity: Great Expectations in Hard Times.* Basingstoke: Palgrave Macmillan, 2016. DOI: 10.1057/9781137522658.0005.

The summer of 2015 brought a succession of negative media headlines and political interventions highlighting concerns about a range of charity issues, including the methods used to raise funds, the salaries of charity chief executives and the sudden closure of 'big brand' charities such as Kids Company. Prime Minister David Cameron spoke of 'frankly unacceptable' actions that damage the reputation of the sector as a whole,[1] and the Chair of the Charity Commission, William Shawcross, described the situation as 'a crisis'.[2] Yet just 12 months previously, in the summer of 2014, media headlines reported on the phenomenal success of the 'ice bucket challenge', which raised over £60 million, largely for research into Motor Neurone disease[3]; the inspirational story of young charity fundraiser Stephen Sutton, who raised over £5 million for the Teenage Cancer Trust[4]; and widespread support for charities' right to campaign, after being told to 'stick to their knitting' by the then-Charities Minister.[5]

Such swings in public opinion exemplify an ambivalent approach to the idea and practice of charity. Despite being a consistent, though often overlooked, feature of life in the UK for centuries, we lack a clear understanding of what charity is, how it operates, who it benefits and what it can and cannot be expected to do. This book has been written to help tackle some misunderstandings and misconceptions of charitable activity in contemporary British society, especially insofar as these affect the thinking of politicians and policymakers. Questions about what charity can or cannot do are of enduring significance, but the need to ask them is sharpened by the context of deep public spending cuts in a period of austerity. There are great expectations that voluntary efforts will arise and expand to plug gaps vacated by the state. Our evidence and analysis raise questions about whether such expectations are realistic – in particular, whether we can expect charitable initiative to respond to needs generated by rising levels of poverty, or whether charitable funds will flow to the most disadvantaged communities.

We begin by asking our central question: is there any logic to charity? Whilst the state is driven by the logic of politics and the demands of voters, and business is driven by the logic of the market and the demands of consumers, what – if anything – is the equivalent logic and driving force behind the charity sector? In Table 1.1, we offer some suggestions about fundamental differences between the dominant logic of the organizing principles and practices of the government and the charity sectors, drawing on a range of concepts from the literature that are discussed further in the chapter.

DOI: 10.1057/9781137522658.0005

TABLE 1.1   *Examples of the different organizing principles in government and charity*

Government	Charity
Systemic provision to meet diverse human needs.	*Idiosyncratic* provision of goods and services as determined by unco-ordinated donor efforts.
Teleological, seeking the 'best' way to organize affairs.	*Non-teleological*, accepting there are many visions of the public good that can be advanced.
Obligatory to fund through compulsory taxation.	*Voluntary* to fund through discretionary donations.
Focus on meeting *basic needs*.	Focus on *needs and human flourishing*.
Categorical constraints mean that political action should ideally benefit all citizens equally.	*Philanthropic particularism* means donors can choose to help only a chosen sub-section of the public.
Spending power constrained by *what will be countenanced by the 'median voter'*.	Spending power constrained by *philanthropic insufficiency*, such that communities lack the capacity or inclination to sustain services through private funding.
Impersonal, delivering services to strangers by paid, professional staff.	*Personal*, delivering services at least in part by volunteers who have, or can build, relationships with clients.
Unified approach within any given period of government to deliver a coherent programme of policies, as set out in a manifesto.	*Disparate approaches* at all times, as different charities pursue different visions of the public good.

The existence of different institutional logics is, of course, known and acknowledged (Scott, 1995). Institutions in different parts of society – the private, state, voluntary and non-profit sectors – have distinctive intra-organizational processes and operate with different belief systems that affect all aspects of those institutions and the people who work within them, including their common practices and definitions of success. But we contend that the nature of the logic that guides charity action – especially that relating to donors' decision-making and the consequent distribution of charitable resources – is not well understood, acknowledged or taken into account by politicians who seek to encourage charity, and to harness it in support of their political programmes.

There are some broader issues that we do not consider in this book because we have chosen to focus on the processes that underpin decisions to support charitable causes and charitable organizations, and on the distribution of those resources. Wider questions that we do not

DOI: 10.1057/9781137522658.0005

explore include: whether the power of philanthropists is justified or not, and how that relates to the source of their wealth (Sayer, 2015); the relationship between philanthropic allocation of resources (especially major donations or substantial endowed foundations) and democracy (Dobkin Hall, 2013; Eikenberry, 2009); the cost of, and justification for, charity tax reliefs (Reich, 2006); and the relationship between philanthropy and public service reform (Ball, 2008; Reich, 2005, 2006).

This chapter begins with a brief historical overview before summarizing some key features of charity in the UK in the twenty-first century, highlighting participation in giving to a variety of cause areas. We then present data on contemporary public attitudes to the role that charity does and should play, and the relationship between private and government funding for different sorts of public goods, exploring the ways in which those attitudes have endured and changed over the past 25 years. We review the main theoretical explanations of why the charity sector exists, none of which necessitates or predicts either a pro-poor bias or an equitable distribution of resources. This introductory chapter concludes by highlighting key issues relating to our current understanding of the logic of charity, which will be explored in greater detail in the body of this book.

Historical overview: charity in a welfare state

In 1948, an opinion poll found that 98 per cent of the British public felt there was no ongoing role for philanthropy because the new institutions of the welfare state had made charity superfluous.[6] Yet six decades later, the ideological narrative of the 'Big Society', and the political reality of public spending cuts in an age of austerity, has put the focus squarely back on the charitable alternative. This shift, from being viewed as superfluous to being viewed as essential, is just one strand in our country's ongoing difficult relationship with the idea and practice of charity.

Even our basic understanding of 'charity' has been – and remains – contested. In 1947 the 'Voluntary Social Service Enquiry', conducted by the social research organization Mass Observation, asked what meaning people attached to the term 'charity'. Answers were characterized as 'complex', 'confusing' and dependent on the respondents' social class and whether they identified more as a donor or as a recipient. 'Charity' was often defined as the transfer of money to organizations helping others, though some also talked of 'doing someone a good turn'. The motivation

DOI: 10.1057/9781137522658.0005

for charity was widely viewed as kindness, generosity and love of fellow people, but others offered a disapproving definition: 'Giving people something for nothing, and I don't believe in it' (Mass Observation, 1947). These dividing lines do not map directly onto political cleavages, despite common perceptions of a closer alignment between Conservative ideologies and voluntarism on one hand and the sometimes dismissive attitudes of Labour politicians on the other. Yet William Beveridge (1948), the architect of the Welfare State – which is often depicted as the nationalization of charity, at least in relation to health, education and basic welfare – clearly envisaged an ongoing role of private, voluntary contribution to the public good:

> '[Voluntary action] is needed to do things which the State is most unlikely to do. It is needed to pioneer ahead of the State and make experiments'.

So at a time, in the late 1940s, when the UK was moving on from charity being the dominant provider of many key services, we find quite conflicting and ambivalent understandings of charity both in the general population and amongst the political class. Almost 60 years later, public opinion on 'charity' continues to lack clarity and agreement – some view it as a moral imperative and essential for maintaining solidarity in an increasingly complex and individualized society, whilst others see it as an unfortunate – and ideally unnecessary – throwback to previous centuries when people could not survive without the whimsical intervention of others. Contemporary attitudes are discussed further in this chapter.

Charity in the twenty-first century: who gives, how and to what causes

Charity is easily dismissed as anachronistic, or as something that is only needed in countries lacking a sufficiently robust welfare state. Yet charitable activity is alive and well in the present era and continues to touch the daily lives of most citizens. Despite a common perception that all public services are organized and paid for by tax-funded arms of the state, they are delivered by organizations that rely to some extent on charitable donations. For example, despite the existence of the National Health Service (NHS), charities working in the field of health (including medical research, hospitals and hospices) are the most popular cause area supported by private donors (CAF, 2015). Further examples of the presence of charitable organizations in spaces assumed to be the

DOI: 10.1057/9781137522658.0005

exclusive preserve of the public sector include charities working in child protection, mental health and education (from pre-school to higher education) as well as charities supporting people with disabilities, working with prisoners and ex-offenders and supporting ex-service men and women and their dependents. Many of the facilities that people encounter and use on a daily basis may now be in public ownership but came into being through charitable initiatives: examples include hospitals, libraries, parks, art galleries, museums, swimming pools and theatres. Contemporary donors continue to facilitate the private funding of a diverse array of activities including the arts, social welfare, medical research and educational provision. However, the embedded nature of charitable effort within the national fabric leaves many recipients unaware of the origins and ongoing income sources of the services and facilities from which they benefit.

Despite a general lack of awareness of the nature and scale of the charitable contribution to modern life, two-thirds (68 per cent) of people describe the role of charities in society as 'highly important' (Glennie and Whillans-Welldrake, 2014, p. 4). This finding is reflected in data published in the most recent edition of the UK Giving survey (CAF, 2015): 70 per cent of British adults report donating money to charity at some point during 2014, with 44 per cent doing so in a typical month. Women were more likely to donate (43 per cent in a typical month, versus 38 per cent of men), though the average monthly donations of men were slightly larger, at £41 versus £36. Cash is the most common form of giving, with over half (55 per cent) of donors making cash donations in 2014, compared to giving by direct debit (30 per cent), playing charitable raffles and lotteries (27 per cent), participating in fundraising events (19 per cent) and writing cheques (9 per cent). While online and text giving are growing in popularity, they remain for now relatively minor in terms of the volume of funding (CAF, 2015). Tax reliefs to individual donors – principally Gift Aid, which is available on all donations made by income taxpayers – have grown substantially, both in terms of the numbers of donors claiming the relief and the total value: from a total cost to the Exchequer of £110 million in 1994–95, to almost £1.2 billion in 2014–15[7] (HM Revenue and Customs, 2015).

There are over 160,000 registered charities in England and Wales, almost 24,000 in Scotland, and an uncertain number, estimated at between 7,000 and 12,000, in Northern Ireland, where a Charity Commission (separate from the one for England and Wales) has only recently begun to compile

DOI: 10.1057/9781137522658.0005

a register.[8] Our statistics refer to England and Wales, but we note that a somewhat more inclusive set of eligibility criteria in Scotland mean that the numbers of registered charities are larger relative to population. Most charities are small and run entirely by volunteers. However, one in twenty (6 per cent) have an annual income over £500,000, and this small fraction accounts for the vast majority (89 per cent) of total voluntary sector income (NCVO, 2015).

If we measure the volume of charitable activity in terms of the numbers of registered charities, there is long-term stability and some signs of recent increases. Over the period since the Register of Charities was established in its modern form (1961) there has been steady expansion but much of this reflects administrative processes, as more organizations have been deemed eligible for charitable status. In the past 20 years the numbers have stabilized – according to the Charity Commission's Annual Reports there have been around 3.3 charities per 1,000 population since the mid-1990s.

We have reliable financial information for large numbers of individual charities from the late 1990s, and analyses show that the median expenditure (not the mean, which is heavily influenced by large outliers) of charities on the Register has been more variable, but also shows a steady increase in the past decade (Lindsey et al., forthcoming, chapter 3). These indicators demonstrate the health and vitality of the charity sector over the recent period. Registration statistics are not a perfect guide. Some growth reflects changing registration criteria (at least one commentator mistook a dramatic increase in the numbers in the early 1990s for a sudden upturn, which actually reflected the results of the Charities Acts of that time, which required many more organizations to register) but the general point holds. At the same time, the logic of an ongoing process of charity formation leads to criticisms of proliferation and duplication.

Registered charities work in a wide range of fields. There are 13 categories of 'charitable purpose' defined in the 2006 Charities Act, as set out in Table 1.2. These categories replace the previous four 'heads of charity' (poverty, education, religion and 'other') which were established over 400 years previously, in the Statute of Charitable Uses 1601. The 13 categories are highly diverse and allow individuals to support almost any cause they wish. There is very little that is actually excluded from this list, although public benefit tests generally prevent charities being set up to serve only their own members, which has been interpreted (e.g., by Brenton, 1985, p. 97) as excluding forms of voluntary action deemed to

TABLE 1.2   *Charitable purposes for the public benefit as defined in the 2006 Charities Act*

1. The prevention or relief of poverty
2. The advancement of education
3. The advancement of religion
4. The advancement of health or the saving of lives
5. The advancement of citizenship or community development
6. The advancement of the arts, culture, heritage or science
7. The advancement of amateur sport
8. The advancement of human rights, conflict resolution or reconciliation or the promotion of religious or racial harmony or equality and diversity
9. The advancement of environmental protection or improvement
10. The relief of those in need, by reason of youth, age, ill-health, disability, financial hardship or other disadvantage
11. The advancement of animal welfare
12. The promotion of the efficiency of the armed forces of the Crown, or of the efficiency of the police, fire and rescue services or ambulance services
13. Any other charitable purposes not covered by the other descriptions of purposes and any new charitable purposes that may be recognized in the future as being similar to another charitable purpose

be more characteristic of working-class communities, though these tests have also been viewed as putting pressure on private schools to create public benefit beyond that experienced by their fee-paying pupils (Baker et al., 2012, p. 11).

According to UK Giving 2015 (CAF, 2015), the causes supported by the largest proportion of individual donors are medical research (supported by 33 per cent of donors), children and young people (30 per cent) and hospitals and hospices (25 per cent). But religious causes received the largest share of the value of donations, as shown in Table 1.3.

Charities receive funding from a variety of public and private sources, with philanthropic donations being only a part of the mix. Organizations need to be assured of future income from diverse funding streams, so that if one declines they can continue with their work. Therefore the composition of income sources is a crucial factor in understanding which charities will survive, let alone thrive, in a period of budget cuts. This is discussed further in Chapters 2 and 3.

Given the typically 'mixed economy' of charity income, focusing solely, or largely, on encouraging support from private donors is therefore an insufficient strategy. Such strategies can also misfire, because what may be logical at the individual level is not necessarily logical at the societal level. Charitable giving does not happen in a vacuum, so

TABLE 1. 3   *The popularity of charitable causes, as reflected in proportion of donors supporting each cause, and proportion of total amount received by each cause*

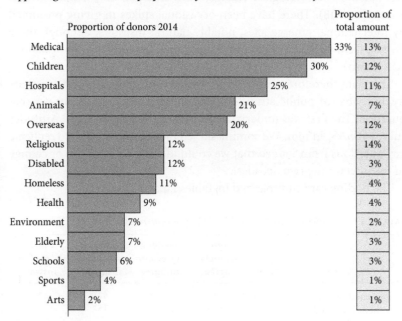

	Proportion of donors 2014	Proportion of total amount
Medical	33%	13%
Children	30%	12%
Hospitals	25%	11%
Animals	21%	7%
Overseas	20%	12%
Religious	12%	14%
Disabled	12%	3%
Homeless	11%	4%
Health	9%	4%
Environment	7%	2%
Elderly	7%	3%
Schools	6%	3%
Sports	4%	1%
Arts	2%	1%

Base: all donating money in the last four weeks (2,252)

Source: CAF, 2015.

Reproduced with the kind permission of CAF (Charities Aid Foundation).

people's private, voluntary philanthropic decisions are influenced by social structures and contexts. How donors choose charities, and how their decisions are influenced by charitable intermediaries, is discussed further in Chapters 4 and 5.

Attitudes to charitable giving and fundraising over time: 1991 and 2015

Thanks to regular social surveys we now know a great deal about who gives to charity, how much they give and the causes they support. There is relative stability both in the proportions of the population that give to charity, and in the amount of funds raised, although there are also recent suggestions of cohort variations (e.g., a decline in generosity across

DOI: 10.1057/9781137522658.0005

cohorts; Smith, 2012). New forms of charitable giving, including those facilitated by technological change, have emerged or expanded (CAF, 2014, pp. 17–18). There have been occasional spikes in giving prompted by international emergencies, notably natural disasters, although these do not seem to have resulted in a substantial upward shift in donations (CAF, 2011).

This data therefore suggests widespread and stable support for charity, but what of public attitudes? Two surveys can help us answer that question. The first was undertaken as part of the British Social Attitudes survey (BSAS) in 1991. We commissioned the second, in 2015, to replicate key questions from 1991 so that we could identify continuities or change in the intervening two decades.

The findings are summarized in Tables 1.4 and 1.5.

TABLE 1.4   *Attitudes to charity and the role of government, 1991 and 2015*

	Year	Agree strongly/ agree	Neither agree nor disagree	Disagree/ strongly disagree	Can't choose/no answer
People should look after themselves and not rely on charities	1991	28%	25%	43%	4%
	2015	52%	33%	15%	
It is NOT everyone's responsibility to give what they can to charities	1991	60%	18%	18%	3%
	2015	48%	28%	24%	
There are so many charities that it is difficult to decide which to give to	1991	77%	10%	10%	3%
	2015	81%	12%	7%	
Most charities are wasteful in their use of funds	1991	36%	33%	24%	7%
	2015	39%	38%	23%	
Government should do less for the needy and encourage charities to do more instead	1991	6%	12%	77%	4%
	2015	9%	27%	64%	
We should support more charities which benefit people in Britain, rather than people overseas	1991	56%	17%	24%	4%
	2015	58%	30%	12%	

Source: 1991 BSAS – self-completion module on public attitudes
(N = 1,212); 2015 – authors' online survey (N = 1,059).

DOI: 10.1057/9781137522658.0005

TABLE 1.5   *Attitudes to responsibility for meeting needs, 1991 and 2015*

	Year	Entirely/ mainly from government	Shared equally	Entirely/ mainly charity	Don't know/ no answer (includes response 'from elsewhere'
Kidney machines	1991	93%	5%	1%	1%
	2015	76%	17%	2%	4%
Housing for homeless people	1991	86%	9%	2%	3%
	2015	65%	26%	5%	3%
Lifeboats	1991	65%	21%	12%	3%
	2015	57%	29%	11%	3%
Protecting rare animals	1991	30%	36%	27%	6%
	2015	19%	40%	35%	5%
Holidays for disabled people	1991	31%	34%	30%	4%
	2015	11%	26%	52%	10%
Food aid to poor countries	1991	29%	34%	30%	6%
	2015	19%	34%	58%	10%

Source: 1991 BSAS – self-completion module on public attitudes
(N = 1,212); 2015 – authors' online survey (N = 1,059)

In 1991, the BSAS found that over three-quarters (77 per cent) of people disagreed with the view that governments 'should do less for the needy and encourage charities to do more instead'. As 15 per cent gave a neutral answer, only 6 per cent supported a smaller role for government in alleviating need. By 2015, there was a small-scale shift in the position: 64 per cent disagreed, 27 per cent had a neutral view and 9 per cent were in some measure of agreement. We find further evidence of these shifts in relation to specific issues.

Both surveys asked respondents whether government, charities or 'both' should be responsible for funding the six areas of expenditure listed in Table 1.4. In both 1991 and 2015 the two areas where the public most strongly believes that responsibility for funding rests entirely or mainly with government were health (represented by 'paying for kidney machines') and 'housing for homeless people', but in both cases the proportions fell, from 93 per cent to 76 per cent and from 86 per cent to 65 per cent, respectively. However, the shift was in favour of viewing these expenditures as a shared responsibility between government and voluntary initiative, as the proportions arguing that responsibility should rest entirely or mainly with charity remained small in both cases, at less than 5 per cent.

DOI: 10.1057/9781137522658.0005

In 1991, two-thirds of people (65 per cent) felt that the financing of lifeboats should be entirely or mainly the responsibility of government, but that proportion dropped to 57 per cent by 2015. In fact, this is an area strongly associated with charitable endeavour. The Royal National Lifeboat Institution (RNLI) is one of the ten largest charities in England and Wales, when ranked by levels of fundraising from individuals, and it has always prided itself on raising money from the community, and not accepting funding from government.

Animal charities can be the butt of criticisms of the capricious nature of charitable giving (Brookes, 2010). The specific question asked in this attitudinal research, though, concerns the protection of rare animals. It is likely that this question has become more salient in the public's mind in the past 25 years, as a result of growing awareness both of environmental issues and of specific threats to rare species in fragile environments. But the public does not regard this as a priority for government. In 1991, just under a third (30 per cent) suggest that funding for the protection of rare animals was wholly or entirely the responsibility of government, but that proportion had dropped to a fifth (19 per cent) by 2015. Now, just over a third (35 per cent) agree that needs in this area should be met entirely or mainly by charity.

In the final two fields of activity – holidays for disabled people and food aid to poor countries – we see strong evidence that a majority of respondents now believe that responsibility rests in the province of charity. In both cases, the proportion favouring charitable finance has gone up from 30 per cent to over a half (52 per cent and 58 per cent, respectively). There has been a substantial reduction in the proportion who believe that holidays for people with disabilities should be entirely or mainly funded by government (31 per cent to 11 per cent), while only 19 per cent now believe that food aid to poor countries should be entirely/mainly the responsibility of government, compared to 29 per cent in 1991.

This latter finding is consistent with responses to the final question about whether charitable support should be directed to people living in Britain rather than overseas. It is also consistent with an analysis of the UK Public Opinion Monitor, which found a majority (more than 64 per cent) believe the UK government should prioritize tackling poverty at home over tackling poverty in other parts of the world (Lindstrom and Henson, 2011, p. 7). It is possible that public awareness of the rise of food banks in the UK may also be driving responses to the question on food aid, since food poverty is now a visible social problem in a way that was not the case 25 years ago.

In 1991, over three-quarters (77 per cent of respondents agreed or strongly agreed with the statement that 'there are so many charities that it is difficult to decide which to give to'. The corresponding proportion in 2015 was higher, at 81 per cent. The proportion of the population agreeing with the statement that 'most charities are wasteful in their use of funds' had also increased slightly, from 36 per cent to 39 per cent. The 2015 survey came at a time when politicians and the media were strongly challenging aspects of the charitable sector, and it is hard to avoid the conclusion that these attacks have had a political character. High salaries of charity staff have persistently attracted criticism, sometimes accompanied by deliberate attempts to associate the payment of such salaries with the receipt of public funding. Such criticisms create in the public mind an aura of extravagance and inefficiency which, at least in the case of high salaries, is at variance with the facts (Mohan and McKay, forthcoming). Nevertheless, the ongoing charge of waste must be disappointing for the charitable sector, given the determined efforts made to improve the measurement of the sector's performance and impact over a number of years. Donors' concerns about charitable efficiency, and how that measure operates as a proxy for general effectiveness in achieving mission, are discussed further in Chapter 4.

Turning to the broader attitudinal questions, the most significant shift in Table 1.4 is in response to the statement that 'people should look after themselves and not rely on charities'. The proportion agreeing with the statement has nearly doubled, from 28 per cent in 1991 to 52 per cent in 2015. This is consistent with wider changes over the same time period in the direction of greater self-reliance and individualism (see, e.g., Bauman, 2000; Beck and Beck-Gernsheim, 2001). The proposition that 'government should do less for the needy and encourage charities to do more instead' is still rejected by a majority of respondents, although the proportion has dropped from 77 per cent to 64 per cent. A specific question on the importance of charitable giving also reveals a shift in attitudes. The 1991 BSA survey invited responses to the proposition that 'it is *not* everyone's responsibility to give what they can to charities' (emphasis in original), and three-fifths (60 per cent) of respondents agreed or strongly agreed. By 2015, this figure was down to 48 per cent, suggesting a growing acceptance of the importance of, and need for, charitable donations.

DOI: 10.1057/9781137522658.0005

The final question asks whether 'we should support more charities which benefit people in Britain, rather than people overseas'. The majority in favour of this statement has barely changed (an increase from 56 to 58 per cent), but the minority that disagree has halved. However, providing more detail on the type of needs being met (e.g., famine relief versus music classes) rather than the location of the recipients might well have produced a more generous response (Barnett and Saxon-Harrold, 1992).

Conclusions on attitudinal data

We highlight five key findings regarding continuity and change in attitudes towards charitable giving from 1991 to 2015. Firstly, there is an enduring belief that 'charity begins at home', but no widespread sense that charity should rise up to replace government, as suggested in some versions of the 'Big Society' idea. This must give pause for thought to those who believe, or hope, that charities can pick up the slack as the state withdraws.

Secondly, a substantial minority continues to hold the view that making a charitable contribution is (and should be) a private, voluntary decision, but there is now a small majority that views giving as an expectation. Thirdly, there is a general view that people should look after themselves and not rely on charities, perhaps indicating that charity is viewed as something that exists for the benefit of 'other people' rather than the reality that most of us are both donors and recipients. Fourthly, the public believe that the charity sector is characterized by a complex proliferation of organizations, rendering it difficult to decide which causes to support; they clearly also have concerns about wastefulness.

Finally, the data shows that people are broadly comfortable with co-production by charity and government for many types of charitable activity. However there remain differential expectations of governmental action in particular areas, such as a greater reliance on government funding for health and rescue (somewhat at variance with the facts in the latter case, which is dominated by charitable funding), and a greater reliance on charitable funding for non-human beneficiaries, geographically distant people and 'nice' rather than 'necessary' spending such as holidays for disabled people.

Whilst this attitudinal data sheds light on public opinion regarding charities, academic study of the sector has generated a number of theories to explain the creation and growth of charitable organizations, to which we now turn.

DOI: 10.1057/9781137522658.0005

Why does the charity sector exist? A review of theoretical approaches

Theoretical approaches explaining the existence of the charity sector can be sorted into two broad types. Firstly, there are theories that focus on the failures of the alternatives (in other words, the state and the market) to optimally produce certain types of goods and services, leaving charity as the only option when the other sectors cannot, will not or do not meet demands (Hansmann, 1980; Salamon, 1987; Weisbrod, 1988). Secondly, there are theories that focus on why in some situations charity has a comparative advantage in supplying goods and services, as a result of being more willing or able to respond to demand and being best-placed to pioneer novel approaches to meeting existing and new needs (Ben-Ner, 1986; Billis and Glennerster, 1998; James, 1983).

Whilst these theories vary in many ways, what matters for our purposes is that no theories explaining the existence of the voluntary sector necessitate a pro-poor bias, and none of them see redistribution as a central role of voluntary organizations. Despite widespread assumptions that 'charity' is synonymous with 'helping the needy', only a small percentage of charities serve those in need as a primary client group. As noted earlier, to qualify for registration as a charity involves proving that the organization promotes at least one of 13 different types of public benefit, which are largely unrelated – and certainly are not necessarily related – to need, poverty, or welfare.

The evidence from the USA is that philanthropy often occurs between individuals of similar socio-economic status and that, counter to common assumptions, 'relatively few non-profit institutions serve the poor as a primary clientele' (Clotfelter, 1992, p. 22). Roberts's 1984 study, which finds less than 10 per cent of giving is 'charitable' as defined in the popular usage of that term, is cited by Jencks (1987, p. 322), who described the inaccuracies inherent in that popular view:

> To most people ... 'charity' conjures up images of the rich helping the poor: medieval Lords endowing almshouses, John D Rockefeller giving away dimes or the average citizen tossing money in a Salvation Army kettle at Christmas. Very few ... [charities] are 'charitable' in that sense. They are almost all meant to 'do good' but the prospective beneficiaries are seldom indigent and are often quite affluent.

Despite public perceptions (Fenton et al., 1993; Ortmann, 1996) charities are not constitutionally bound to be redistributive, with no requirement

DOI: 10.1057/9781137522658.0005

in UK charity law for charities to redistribute from richer to poorer groups. Indeed, funding patterns for voluntary organizations suggest that those working with the most needy recipients are funded primarily by the state (Clifford et al., 2013); this is discussed further in Chapter 2 of this book. However, popular understanding of, and attitudes towards, charitable activity rest to a large extent upon such 'pro-poor' assumptions, and many charities both act and are treated as if they are a vehicle by which the most advantaged in society are able to meet indigent need (Odendahl, 1990; Ortmann, 1996; Wagner, 2000). This misunderstanding is repeatedly evident in political speeches: in the same comments referred to in the opening sentence of this chapter, the Prime Minister also said:

> 'Our charities undertake vital work, bringing communities together and providing support to some of the most vulnerable members of our society'.[9]

Whilst many charities do exactly this sort of work, many do not, either because that is not what they were set up to do or because it is not what their donors fund them to do. And, as shown in Chapter 3, the distribution of neighbourhood charities suggests that many serve to recycle resources *within* communities, rather than making connections *across* communities. The distributional consequences of charitable action across different causes as a result of geography and donor decision-making processes are the foci of this book, because we believe a better understanding of these processes provides illuminating insights into the logic – such that there is – of charity.

Conclusions: the logic of charity and politics

Charity has assumed a renewed significance in public policy in a context of austerity-driven reductions in public expenditure, but in fact governments since at least the Thatcher administrations (1979–1992) have attempted to encourage an expansion of charitable giving to, and provision by, the charitable sector. Much political support has been largely rhetorical or exhortatory, but politicians have taken some practical steps to promote and encourage charity via enabling legislation, financial incentives and other levers available to government (see Kendall and Knapp, 1996, p. 3). Examples include: the introduction of Gift Aid in 1990 (during Margaret Thatcher's final term in office) which gave tax relief

DOI: 10.1057/9781137522658.0005

on certain donations made by taxpayers; the creation of the National Lottery in 1994 during John Major's premiership, which has raised over £34 billion for 'good causes' by 2015; the expansion of Gift Aid in 2000 to apply to all donations made by taxpayers during Tony Blair's time at 10 Downing Street; the Treasury Cross-Cutting Review of the role of the Third Sector during the government led by Gordon Brown; and the Giving White Paper and subsequent reforms to encourage philanthropy, including new tax reliefs for charitable legacies, implemented by the Coalition government led by David Cameron. For data on the annual and cumulative impact of various tax reliefs on charitable giving and charity finances, which were worth c.£3.4 billion in total in 2013–14, see HM Revenue and Customs (2015).

This cross-party political support reflects the generally positive view of charity held by the general public, indicated by majoritarian participation in charitable giving and volunteering, and widespread belief in the importance of charity. In bald terms: the right wing's preferences for 'small government' leads to hopes that charity will step in to meet needs when the state is 'rolled back', and the left's roots in voluntary organizations, notably the trade unions, lead to hopes that charity will foster solidarity, tempered by concerns that charity undermines broader structural reform and advances the interests of richer donors. Yet despite this broad cross-party desire to encourage charitable activity (in particular monetary contributions), and despite both pro-active policy initiatives and the anticipated negative impact of the 2008 financial crash on charitable support, the needle on giving has barely altered either up or down in recent decades, when measured as a percentage of GDP (Sargeant and Shang, 2011, p. 5).

The idea of the 'Big Society' is the latest manifestation of a shared view that more can be done to support and encourage charitable and voluntary initiative. The idea has been criticized, but the underlying principle – that there will be a substantial shift in the balance between state and private initiative – remains central to the Conservative government elected in 2015. All political parties appear to subscribe to the view that charity is broadly a 'good thing', that it can be increased and that it can address otherwise unmet social needs. Yet, as we note earlier, these high expectations are coupled with a low public understanding of charity in both theory and practice. Without an informed understanding of who gives to charity, the processes through which they decide to support particular causes, the distribution of organizations and the pattern of

DOI: 10.1057/9781137522658.0005

funding for charities, policymaking will be based on hopes, assumptions and ideologically driven ideas of what charity is, and how it can be expanded.

This book is a contribution to both a much-needed evidence base and efforts to attain a clearer understanding of the logic of charity. It reviews current knowledge, drawing on a wide range of existing data, and presents a series of original research findings that explore charity and its distribution in contemporary UK society. We have written this book to challenge the general misunderstanding of what 'charity' entails, to shed light on the actual distribution of charitable benefit and to contribute to political debates by arguing that charity is not as malleable in political hands as might be hoped or expected.

Notes

1 https://www.gov.uk/government/news/new-law-to-protect-vulnerable-from-rogue-fundraisers
2 https://www.gov.uk/government/speeches/rathbones-charity-conversations-series-2015-william-shawcross-speech
3 http://www.bbc.co.uk/news/magazine-29013707
4 https://www.teenagecancertrust.org/get-help/young-peoples-stories/stephen-sutton
5 http://www.theguardian.com/society/2014/sep/03/charities-knitting-politics-brook-newmark
6 According to Chesterman (1979), cited in Kendall and Knapp (1996)
7 http://www.civilsociety.co.uk/finance/news/content/20494/caf_and_john_major_hail_60bn_raised_through_gift_aid
8 https://www.gov.uk/government/organisations/charity-commission; http://www.oscr.org.uk; https://www.charitycommissionni.org.uk
9 https://www.gov.uk/government/news/new-law-to-protect-vulnerable-from-rogue-fundraisers

DOI: 10.1057/9781137522658.0005

2

Who Benefits from Charitable Expenditures? The Distribution of Charitable Resources by Cause

Abstract: *Charities may be perceived as organizations that are funded entirely from private donations, but which charitable causes receive funding from which sources of income? This chapter analyses the distribution of the income of the charitable sector by main sphere of activity (charitable causes) and by funding streams (private donations, government, etc.). One particular feature of the logic of charity is the degree of concentration of income in general, and of income from particular funding streams, within relatively small numbers of organizations. Major shifts in the distribution of resources therefore seem unlikely to be achieved – for instance, even small-scale reductions in government funding would require some areas of charitable activity to double their private fundraising – which suggests some challenges in the context of the current shrinkage of the state.*

Mohan, John and Beth Breeze. *The Logic of Charity: Great Expectations in Hard Times.* Basingstoke: Palgrave Macmillan, 2016. DOI: 10.1057/9781137522658.0006.

According to William Shawcross (2012), chair of the Charity Commission for England and Wales since 2012, '[M]ost members of the public, when asked, would say a charity is an organization funded from private donations'. He went on to note the supposed reliance of charities on government. In fact the funding mix of charities is heterogeneous: whilst some do indeed receive nearly all their income from governmental sources, others are almost entirely reliant on private donors, while fees from individuals account for the bulk of the income of some subsectors of the charity population. The balance between private and public initiative, and between donations and fees, has also shifted over time. A mix of income sources has been the norm for many charitable organizations for most of the past century. For instance, the pre-NHS voluntary (charitable) hospitals developed funding streams that entailed payment by individuals (Gorsky et al., 2002; Gorsky and Mohan, 2006). An assessment during the 1930s drew attention to the growth of public funding to charities (Braithwaite, 1938) but, even then, the UK was some decades behind the USA, where government payments to nonprofit institutions were well known from the early twentieth century (Salamon, 1987).

Contemporary discussions of diversification in the funding mix now focus on the theme of 'hybridity' (Billis, 2010). Some charitable organizations, positioned between market, state and community, are characterized by a complex mix of funding from donative sources, fees paid by individuals purchasing services, grants and contracts from government, member subscriptions and so forth. Individual charities are thus characterized by multiple logics: acting in a quasi-commercial manner on the one hand, and in a conventional charitable fashion on the other, depending on the nature of the activities being carried out, the funding streams supporting them and the requirements of funders. For instance, housing associations are charged with providing social housing at below-market rates, but they seek to generate commercial returns from existing assets in order to keep rents down. Hybridity may, however, be a characteristic of a limited subset of organizations because (as we show) some charities are very heavily reliant on specific sources of income, and very little on commercial activities, while others draw on a mix of sources.

In this chapter we investigate the differences in the funding mix of charities across subsectors of the charity population. The picture is much more complex than might be implied by normative utterances that charities are simply bodies funded by private donations. Charities

DOI: 10.1057/9781137522658.0006

use resources derived from various sources in pursuit of their charitable objectives. The existing evidence base tells us much about aggregate patterns in these sources. For example, there are studies of the proportion of the population engaged in giving to charity and the amounts they give, of variations over time and across birth cohorts in household giving (Smith et al., 2011) or of giving to particular causes (Atkinson et al., 2012). Other elements of the funding mix, such as major (greater than £1 million) charitable donations (Breeze, 2012) or grant-making by the UK's largest charitable foundations (Pharoah et al., 2015), have also received attention. These provide informative analyses of significant elements of charitable giving. But they still leave us in the position of the blind people and the elephant: able to identify parts of the beast's anatomy, but unable to comprehend the whole. For instance, the aggregate statistics in the annual *UK Civil Society Almanac* (NCVO, 2015) provide a very broad-brush picture of the income sources of charities, below which there is considerable variation between charitable causes and between individual organizations.

What proportion of the various sources of charitable income goes to which causes, and how does the distribution relate to other sources of funds? To explore these questions, we begin by describing the principal sources of income that charities rely on, consider the logic that lies behind their allocation and then present data to illustrate the distribution of particular income sources across different charitable causes. In a related work, Clifford and Mohan (forthcoming) break this picture down still further, looking at organization-level variations.

This analysis contributes to important debates about the shape and identity of the charity sector, in which perceptions have been shaped by prominent statements about what the distribution ought to be. As well as Shawcross's observations, there have been arguments about the degree of concentration of charitable resources in certain large organizations, whether or not this concentration is at the expense of funding for smaller charities, and criticisms that the degree of public funding received by charities compromises their independence. The subtext appears to be that the only 'true' form of charitable organization is one which receives no public money, and indeed relies entirely on philanthropic donations from individuals. As we show, that would leave a very small charitable sector indeed, and one with a much narrower spectrum of activity. Whether that is the kind of charitable sector we would wish to see is a matter of debate.

DOI: 10.1057/9781137522658.0006

The income sources of large English and Welsh charities

We draw upon sample data for the financial year 2009–10 for some 7,000 English and Welsh charities having incomes greater than £500,000: the threshold at which, because of the reporting requirements of charities of this size, we can expect robust and consistent classification of financial information (Morgan, 2010, 2011) in accordance with the Statement of Recommended Practice (SORP) prepared by the Charity Commission. The sample is representative of charities which, collectively, account for over 90 per cent of total incoming resources of English and Welsh charities.

Even so, there is the potential for ambiguity. Charitable organizations summarize their income under a set of headings which are reasonably general in character, such as 'voluntary income', 'charitable activities' or 'activities generating funds'. The public may understand the first of these to mean donations, and the latter as income from fundraising, but it is not always easy to identify genuinely 'philanthropic' income. As an instance of this, membership fees could be included under voluntary income if accountants held that they constituted a donation rather than something conveying entitlement to a service. Do members of the National Trust, for example, perceive their annual fee as a charitable donation or as something which gives them an entitlement to receive services in the form of admission to National Trust properties?

To overcome these challenges we analyse data generated by collaborative work with the National Council for Voluntary Organizations (NCVO), in the course of which procedures have been developed for classifying the accounts data (see Kane et al., 2013) in a manner which allows us to identify six major categories of income:

1   *Fundraising from individuals.* Asking is as old as giving, and therefore found throughout history (Mullin, 2007, p. 9; Sargeant and Jay, 2014, p. 2), but the novelty of organized fundraising is the role of intermediaries to arrange the transfer of resources between strangers (Zunz, 2011; see also Chapter 5). Recent decades have seen the growth of vigorous forms of fundraising aided by emerging technologies, including direct mail, 'red button' television appeals, telethons (lengthy TV broadcasts involving celebrities) and web-based technologies (Scharf et al., 2015). In this chapter, we identify income from individuals in the form of donations and

DOI: 10.1057/9781137522658.0006

legacies, which also includes income from Gift Aid claims, and membership subscriptions where charity accounts suggest that these are, in substance, donations rather than payment for goods or services. We also identify income from individuals through the trading or other fundraising activities carried out by a charity primarily to generate incoming resources that will be used to undertake its charitable activities.

2   *Income from fees paid by individuals.* We identify income from individuals in the form of payments for goods and services provided for the benefit of the charity's beneficiaries. The largest single element here is fees paid for private education.

3   *Government funding.* Government funding of charities has always involved a mixture of grants and contracts, although the latter are very much in the ascendancy in the second decade of the twenty-first century. Many public agencies are involved in funding charities, from EU-funded programmes down to town and parish councils.

4   *Income from investments.* Internally generated income, from investments, endowments and property, constitutes a further element of the income mix, albeit one which depends either on the historical accumulation of assets or on the largesse of a major donor. Some charities exist as grant-making bodies to fund others from their endowments, which are often based on an 'in perpetuity' model (distributing the investment and preserving the capital), though the idea of impermanent 'spend out' and 'flow through' models are gaining appeal, especially amongst donors seeking to tackle more urgent problems such as developing new vaccines (Institute for Philanthropy, 2010).

5   *Income from the voluntary sector and National Lottery.* This includes grants from charitable trusts, services provided under contract to other voluntary organizations and grants from National Lottery distributors. Lotteries have long been used to generate funds whilst providing players the chance to win a prize. The most significant of these is the UK National Lottery, launched in 1994, with 28 per cent of the purchase price of Lottery tickets going to 'good causes' – by 2015, the scheme had raised £34 billion to support almost half a million projects.[1]

6   *Miscellaneous and smaller sources.* These include the private sector, and also trading subsidiaries established to generate surpluses for charities.

DOI: 10.1057/9781137522658.0006

All the sources of income summarized here have different underlying logics. Spontaneous gifts in response to street collections, or requests from friends to sponsor a parachute jump or mountain climb, are not likely to be the product of extensive reflection and will be influenced by social norms such as peer pressure and reciprocity. By contrast, decisions about leaving large charitable bequests, or making million-pound donations during a donor's lifetime, are the product of much longer and more complex thought processes, often involving professional intermediaries such as fundraisers and philanthropy advisers (Breeze and Lloyd, 2013).

Funding for charities from public sector agencies will be associated with a consideration of levels of social need, the merits of the distinctive ways in which charities provide services and the comparative costs of providers of public services. Whether or not any given charity receives funds from grant-making trusts will reflect factors such as the eligibility criteria for a particular funding stream, and the perspective and preferences of current trustees. As a competitive process it will also reflect organizations' ability to generate effective applications. And corporate sponsorship must inevitably reflect the distribution and priorities of corporate entities (at least insofar as it entails direct linkages between beneficiary organizations and the companies making the donations).

These underlying logics do not all point in the same direction, although there is a great deal of evidence pointing towards substantial concentration of charitable funds. So when we begin to explore Shawcross's statement that the public assumes that charities rely on private donors, we do indeed find a substantial bedrock of private donations in the income mix of the charitable sector as a whole. Such private sources of income include donations, legacies and income from the endowments and investments of charities. Substantial amounts are generated in this way – individual donations to English and Welsh charities are estimated at around £10 billion per annum, with a further £2 billion received by charities in the form of legacies in a typical year, as well as some £3 billion in investment income from charities' assets (NCVO, 2015). We also find considerable variations both between charitable causes and between individual charitable organizations.

Our interest is in the extent to which charities rely on philanthropic sources of income, and the distribution of such income across subsectors of the charity population. We also investigate the degree of concentration of such income (e.g., does a small set of charitable organizations account for the greater part of resources?) and variations in the distribution of charitable resources between geographical areas (see Chapter 3).

DOI: 10.1057/9781137522658.0006

The income sources of English and Welsh charities

The emphasis here is principally on philanthropic income, and on its distribution across causes and across individual organizations. However, comparisons are made with other sources, such as fees paid by individuals, and government funding.

Shares of charitable resources and shares of income sources

The income of charitable organizations in England and Wales amounted to some £57 billion in 2009–10, which, to put it in context, equated to rather more than half of total expenditure on the NHS. In Table 2.1, we consider the distribution of total income across different causes, and the contribution of various income sources across charitable causes. We use the International Classification of Nonprofit Organizations (ICNPO), originally devised for comparative purposes (Salamon and Anheier, 1996, 1997), in acknowledgement that most nonprofit organizations are clustered within a small number of subsets of economic activity within the Standard Industrial Classification (education, health, housing and international development).

The six sources of income identified here generated approximately £48 billion in the 2009–10 financial year for our sampled organizations. Five causes accounted for just over half (51 per cent) of the total: primary and secondary education (16 per cent), social services (13 per cent), housing (8.6 per cent), religious congregations (7.2 per cent) and international development charities (6.8 per cent). Compared to Table 1.3, an obvious absentee is charities related to medicine and health, which are very popular among donors; the reason is that various subsets of health-related activity are separated in the analysis given here. If aggregated, health charities would account for a further 13.5 per cent of total income received by charities.

Here, we indicate the proportions of the sector's total income received by each ICNPO category, broken down by funding source (Table 2.2). For clarity, the table is restricted to the classes of the ICNPO that either receive at least £1 billion in total funding (or just over 2 per cent of the total), or have at least one element of their income equivalent to at least 1 per cent of the total. We also show only those subsectors in which at least 1 per cent of total sectoral resources are derived from a particular source. The 14 subsectors of the ICNPO that are included collectively account for over five-sixths of the total income of registered charities.

DOI: 10.1057/9781137522658.0006

TABLE 2.1 *Breakdown by ICNPO categories of income; shares of income by funding source and ICNPO category*

International classification of nonprofit organizations	Income from fundraising (£m)	Fees paid by individuals (£m)	Government (£m)	Voluntary sector (incl. Lottery) (£m)	Internally generated (£m)	Business, other sources (£m)	Total income (£m)	Share of total income (%)
Primary and secondary education	234	5209	1890	145	191	77	7740	16.1
Social services	1440	504	3690	288	186	156	6270	13.1
Housing	249	2022	1530	78	182	81	4140	8.6
Religious congregations	1420	557	360	459	491	167	3460	7.2
International activities	1090	168	1370	437	41	161	3270	6.8
Culture/arts	349	741	1070	339	209	121	2820	5.9
Grant-making foundations	811	92	219	136	749	214	2220	4.6
Employment/training	53	76	1050	69	24	404	1670	3.5
Medical research	942	16	93	55	286	253	1650	3.4
Hospitals/rehabilitation	465	750	140	40	68	37	1500	3.1
Other health services	309	127	418	523	39	47	1460	3.0
Nursing homes	507	78	544	46	62	20	1260	2.6
Environment	284	358	280	108	92	76	1200	2.5
Other education	37	214	619	57	31	68	1030	2.1

Note: The table shows only those ICNPO categories which account for at least 2% of total income.

Source: Author's calculations from charity accounts data.

DOI: 10.1057/9781137522658.0006

TABLE 2.2 *Share of total sector income accounted for by particular combinations of subsector and funding stream*

ICNPO subsector	Fundraising	Fees paid by individuals	Government	Voluntary sector (incl. Lottery)	Internally generated	Share of sector total
Primary and secondary education		10.8	3.9			16.1
Social services	3.0	1.0	7.7			13.1
Housing		4.2	3.2			8.6
Religious congregations	3.0	1.2		1.0	1.0	7.2
International activities	2.3		2.9			6.8
Culture/arts		1.5	2.2			5.9
Grant-making foundations	1.7				1.6	4.6
Employment/training			2.2			3.5
Medical research	2.0					3.4
Hospitals/rehabilitation	1.0	1.6				3.1
Other health services				1.1		3.0
Nursing homes	1.1		1.1			2.6
Environment						2.5
Other education			1.3			2.1

Note: The causes included here account for 83% of total income of registered charities in England and Wales. Thus primary and secondary education accounts for 16.1% of the total and fees paid by individuals to such charities accounts for 10.8% of total income. For clarity, only those combinations of subsector and funding stream are identified which account for at least 1% of the total.

Source: Author's calculations from charity accounts data.

The largest single element of funding to the charitable sector, account-ing for just under 11 per cent of the total, was fees paid by individuals to private educational establishments. A further 4 per cent of total income was accounted for by government fees to private education – in other words, payments to academies, which are independent of government but which exist to provide alternatives to state-controlled schools. The second largest contribution, at 7.7 per cent, was payments by government to social services charities. Rents paid by individuals to housing associa-tions formed 4.2 per cent of the sector's total income, with a further 3.2 per cent being payments by government to housing associations.

Therefore, the five largest individual components of income for the charitable sector, accounting for 30 per cent of its incoming resources, took the form either of fees paid by individuals or payments by the government for the delivery of services. This suggests two things. Firstly, charities do not, if they ever did, rely solely on private donations from individuals or businesses (or upon the income generated by endow-ments which were the product of such generosity). Secondly, it is more informative to emphasize variations across charitable causes, rather than to consider aggregates such as the proportion of the sector's income which is derived from one source or another.

These figures clearly demonstrate that different subgroups of the charity population have quite different income profiles. The largest single contributions from individuals in the form of donations and legacies were to social service charities and to religious organizations, each of which received over 3 per cent of the total income of charities. Contributions of over 2 per cent of the total were also made by govern-ment to organizations working in the fields of arts and culture, employ-ment and training, and international development. The charitable causes and income sources highlighted in Table 2.2 account for just under half of total incoming resources for the charitable sector.

Reflecting these variations, we consider the distribution of income sources *across causes* (Table 2.3), to investigate which causes attract the largest proportions of particular funding streams. Unsurprisingly, primary and secondary education is the destination of some 40 per cent of fees paid by individuals to charitable organizations, followed by 16 per cent for housing (i.e., rents). Nearly 60 per cent of government fund-ing to the charitable sector goes to social services, housing, primary and secondary education, employment and training, and international development. The largest shares of donative funding go to various health

TABLE 2.3 *Share of each source of income going to each cause*

ICNPO Subsector	Income from Fundraising	Fees paid by individuals	Government	Voluntary sector (incl Lottery)	Internal	Business, other sources	Share of total income
Primary and Secondary Education	2.3	**41.5**	**11.7**	4.2	**5.7**	3.0	16.1
Social Services	**14.4**	4.0	**22.9**	**8.4**	**5.6**	**6.1**	13.1
Housing	2.5	**16.1**	**9.5**	2.3	**5.5**	3.1	8.6
Religious congregations	**14.2**	4.4	2.2	**13.4**	**14.8**	**6.5**	7.2
International activities	**10.9**	1.3	**8.5**	**12.8**	1.2	**6.2**	6.8
Culture / arts	3.5	**5.9**	**6.6**	**9.9**	**6.3**	4.7	5.9
Grantmaking foundations	**8.1**	0.7	1.4	4.0	**22.5**	**8.3**	4.6
Employment / training	0.5	0.6	**6.5**	2.0	0.7	**15.7**	3.5
Medical research	**9.4**	0.1	0.6	1.6	**8.6**	**9.8**	3.4
Hospitals / rehabilitation	4.6	**6.0**	0.9	1.2	2.0	1.4	3.1
Other health services	3.1	1.0	2.6	**15.3**	1.2	1.8	3.0
Nursing homes	**5.1**	0.6	3.4	1.3	1.9	0.8	2.6
Environment	2.8	2.8	1.7	3.2	2.8	2.9	2.5
Other education	0.4	1.7	3.8	1.7	0.9	2.6	2.1

Note: Only those causes with at least 2% of total sector resources included. Highlighted cells indicate causes attracting at least 5% of the relevant income source

Source: Author's calculations from charity accounts.

DOI: 10.1057/9781137522658.0006

charities, international development and religious organizations, reflecting the continued popular appeal of such causes.

What of those causes that attract very little philanthropic funding? Mental health, economic, social and community development, employment and training, and law and legal services are all fields of activity that receive less than 1 per cent of funds donated by individuals. Yet to take one example: mental health is regarded as a significant and urgent policy priority, costing businesses and taxpayers hundreds of billions of pounds each year, but it clearly attracts little philanthropic support, notwithstanding the fact that it has always been relatively underfunded within the NHS by comparison with other areas of health care (Royal College of Psychiatrists, 2009). The other fields named earlier are characterized by the kinds of market failures discussed in Chapter 1, which are theorized to explain the origins of the charity sector, but it is obvious that philanthropists have not chosen to step in to plug the gap. The rapid withdrawal of public funds from some of these areas – for example, law and legal services – will be a test case for whether philanthropists are willing to step into the breach for fields of activity that have been very reliant upon public money.

The funding profile of individual charitable causes also varies greatly. We consider, for each of the main groups of the ICNPO classification, cases in which the proportion of total income received from a particular source is either at least 25 per cent or is in the majority. The threshold of 25 per cent is also used by Clifford and Mohan (forthcoming) in their analysis of organization-level variations, to characterize what they regard as a 'substantial' income source. We find there are only three classes of charitable organizations in our sample in which the majority of funding comes from private donations or legacies: medical research (57 per cent), emergency relief (70 per cent), and animal welfare (71 per cent). Fees paid by individuals constitute the largest single component of the income of charities operating in primary or secondary education (67 per cent), and the proportion for hospitals and rehabilitation services is approximately 50 per cent.

There are then seven subsectors in which the majority of income comes from government. The highest proportion is mental health charities (77 per cent); the others include 'other education' (mainly further or adult education provision: 60 per cent), social services (59 per cent), economic, social and community development (56 per cent), employment and training (63 per cent), legal services (61 per cent) and what is known in the ICNPO schema as 'other philanthropic intermediaries and voluntarism promotion' (54 per cent). These are entities such as

DOI: 10.1057/9781137522658.0006

local Councils for Voluntary Service, which have received considerable government support to enable them to deliver functions of matching volunteers with potential volunteering opportunities, and providing advice and support to local voluntary organizations.

The other subsectors referred to here have long been recipients of government funding, certainly since the term of office of the Thatcher government, which significantly expanded the voluntary sector's role in dealing with mass unemployment (Brenton, 1985; Kramer, 1990; Lewis, 1993). Other fields of activity in which individual donations and legacies are important, accounting for at least 25 per cent of income in the individual subsectors, include hospitals and rehabilitation services, nursing homes (including hospices), civic and advocacy charities, international development and religious charities.

We briefly explore the distribution of legacy income in more detail. Since making a bequest requires a conscious decision, embodied in a will, it also implies that individuals have made a considered assessment of their charitable priorities. Therefore, analyses of the distribution of legacy income, and also the way in which the distribution differs from that of other forms of charitable income, offer some important insights into the impact of charitable giving.

On average, some £2 billion per annum is received by English and Welsh charities in the form of legacies. Various organizations (English universities, various national museums and galleries) which do not appear on the register of charities are estimated to receive perhaps a further £200 million from legacies. By way of comparison, Inland Revenue statistics on the total value of estates at death suggest that in any given year, individuals leave in excess of £50 billion (Atkinson, 2013). Thus charitable legacies to charities in any given year equate to approximately 3 per cent of the total value of estates. This proportion is considerably higher than estimates of the proportion of household income given to charity, which typically equates to around 0.5 per cent.

There is considerable variation between charities in the likelihood of receiving legacy income. In four categories of the ICNPO, more than half of the charities in our sample did so: animal protection (83 per cent); nursing homes, hospitals and rehabilitation (both 70 per cent); and medical research (58 per cent). Conversely, fewer than 10 per cent of charities in the fields of law and legal services, economic, social and community development, and employment and training received legacies.

Approximately half of all legacy income received by English and Welsh charities accrues to three categories of charity: medical research, a

DOI: 10.1057/9781137522658.0006

broad social services category and animal protection. This – particularly the latter – may well accord with popular perceptions of the destination of charitable funds. Seven-figure bequests to animal charities have certainly received media coverage but such bequests are rare. Other fields of activity receiving more than 5 per cent of the total were nursing homes, hospitals and rehabilitation, religious organizations and emergency and relief charities, followed by international development (4.7 per cent).

While five out of six charities in the field of animal protection receive legacies, this is not a large field of charitable activity (with the exception of a small number of very large organizations), so this equates to around 200 charities. In addition, we should also consider the relative size of the legacy income received by these organizations, as well as the distribution within each subsector. A small number of animal protection charities – examples might be the Royal Society for the Prevention of Cruelty to Animals (RSPCA), the People's Dispensary for Sick Animals (PDSA) and the Royal Society for the Protection of Birds (RSPB) – dominate the legacy market, regularly receiving in excess of £10 million per annum in this way. While a high proportion of animal welfare charities receive legacies, most are small nature reserves or wildlife trusts.

This analysis serves to demonstrate the heterogeneity of charitable organizations and their funding. Discussion about the distribution of charitable resources can sometimes fixate on particular issues (large individual donations to particular organizations, or the likelihood that certain subsectors of the charity population are more or less likely to receive income from specific sources) at the expense of consideration of the whole picture. Legacies are a particularly good example but we have also shown variations in the distribution of other income sources across subsets of the charity population.

Concentration of resources and size of charitable organization

These analyses are for broad categories of charitable causes, and there are large numbers of organizations in each class. What about the concentration of resources in small numbers of organizations and organization-level variations in the distribution?

There have been discussions about the size distribution of charitable organizations, and about the apparent high levels of concentration of funding in some organizations. Most charities are small: while the mean expenditure of English and Welsh charities is around £400,000, the

DOI: 10.1057/9781137522658.0006

median (the midpoint of the distribution, when ranked) is £13,000. An expenditure of £300,000 would place a charity in the top 10 per cent of organizations; £800,000 would secure entry to the top 5 per cent; and only organizations with expenditures greater than £6.5 million would feature in the top 1 per cent by size.

Proponents of voluntary action often make reference to the advantages of small, local organizations in terms of personal knowledge of those being supported by charities, and in terms of knowledge of the local context in which charities operate (Billis and Glennerster, 1998). Consider, for example, David Green's evocation of the manner in which the friendly societies, pioneers of the provision of sick pay and unemployment insurance, were able both to identify emerging needs and, through close personal contact, minimize fraud (Green, 1993). Equally, there are fields of charitable endeavour in which scale is clearly essential – consider the mobilization of resources for international development causes, where an ability to operate at a large scale is a prerequisite for being able to reach needy communities in a cost-effective manner. In contrast, a small volunteer-led UK-based charity focusing on a very local area might need limited funding to enable it to fulfil its objectives.

There is clearly a tension between these views of the sector. Can the responsiveness to need that is provided by small local charities be combined with efficient service delivery that provides a cost-effective and innovative solution to social challenges? The question has attracted attention for a number of years. Knight's (1993) widely known investigations identified a process of bifurcation in the charitable sector, between large, professionalized organizations whose principal focus was on delivering government services, and small, local organizations. He saw this as a desirable development that was to be encouraged. The NCVO *Almanac*, which began publication around the same time, has adopted a shorthand for classification of charities by size, based on income bands arranged in powers of £10 (£1,000–£9,999, £10,000–£99,999 and so on). Since the mid-1990s, this classification has consistently shown that large organizations account for an increased share of the quantum of resources of registered charities. It oversimplifies the process of concentration of charity income over time, since it can easily lead to the conclusion that large charities are growing at the expense of small ones. Essentially, if calculations are based on the place of charities in the income distribution (e.g., arbitrarily defined income bands), it is inevitable that larger organizations will accrue a greater share of resources, because there is no upper limit in the top band (£100 million plus) and the further up the

DOI: 10.1057/9781137522658.0006

income distribution one goes, the more scope that organizations have for growing while remaining within the same income band.

Such evidence has been used to argue that the concentration of resources in the sector is undesirable. For example, Nick Seddon, formerly of the think-tanks Civitas and Reform, and an advisor to David Cameron since 2013, criticized the rise of 'super-charities', asserting that the concentration of income in the largest charities was indubitably 'becoming more acute over time' (Seddon, 2007, pp. 95–102. This is premised on analysis of change over only two financial years in the income distribution of the top 1,000 fundraising charities. Similar comments were prominent in publications from the Centre for Social Justice (2013, 2014), whose founder, Iain Duncan Smith, had previously criticized the so-called Tescoization of the charitable sector. This phrase arose because the former chief executive of the supermarket chain Tesco, Terry Leahy, had responded to criticism that his company had a dominant share in the grocery market in the UK by pointing out that they were still well short of having a majority share, thus leaving plenty of scope for further expansion. Duncan Smith (2005) was worried about similar dominance in the charitable world, deploring the potential 'uniformity of thought and action' of large charities.

However, the argument could be made that size is associated with professionalism and efficiency (as Seddon himself acknowledges (2007, pp. 98–99)). Sir Stephen Bubb, the head of the Association of Chief Executives of Voluntary Organizations (ACEVO) has been prominent here, arguing that charities have grown large because they are good at doing what they do (cited in Backus and Clifford, 2013, p. 762). Size might enable organizations to benefit from large-scale public contracts, or to achieve scale economies in fundraising.

There are several threads in these arguments. Most prominently, there is a concern that the expansion of large charities is at the expense of small ones; a presumed association of size with government funding (and therefore a loss of independence); and a worry that the distinctive features of small charities, in terms of responsiveness and quality of support for vulnerable individuals, are threatened by aggressive encroachment from large national entities. On the first of these points, Backus and Clifford (2013) have challenged the calculations on which claims of so-called Tescoization are based. They show that in fact, if one considers concentration ratios – the share of total resources accruing to the largest organizations (the top 5, 10, 25 and so on) – there is little evidence of increased concentration over time. However, they do demonstrate that the typical small charity has grown rather less than the typical large one, and that

DOI: 10.1057/9781137522658.0006

there is a positive relationship between initial size and growth, suggesting that there are advantages of being a certain size.

But what is the evidence about the concentration of resources in particular charities? We analyse n-charity concentration ratios for this purpose. These are defined as the share of total income going to the n largest charities. We analyse such ratios for the top 5, 10, 25 and 100 charities by funding stream. Table 2.4 shows the results. The most concentrated source is legacy income, in which the largest five organizations ranked by this income source account for 22 per cent of total legacies; nearly half of legacy income in the sector accrues to the 25 largest charities, and two-thirds of it goes to the top 85 organizations. To give an idea of the degree of concentration this implies, if incomes of charities as a whole were as concentrated as is legacy income, it would mean the five largest charities had an average income of £2 billion, whereas as yet no registered charity has breached the £1 billion threshold. Typically the 5-charity concentration ratio for total income is about 5 per cent while the 100-charity ratio is just over one-quarter (26 per cent) of the sector's income.

For comparison, other sources of income are far less concentrated. The 5-charity ratios for individual donations, for fees paid by individuals, and for government income are around half of that observed for legacies (between 11 and 13 per cent), as is the 10-charity ratio, while the ratio for legacy income in the top 25 charities is more than twice that for individual fees, and nearly twice that for government income or for individual donations.

Not only is there concentration of incomes in the charitable sector as a whole, but there is also concentration of incomes from particular funding

TABLE 2.4   *Concentration ratios for principal sources of charity income*

Number of charities for which concentration ratio is calculated	Legacies	Individual donors	Fees from individuals	Government	Internally generated	Total income
5	22.0	10.9	12.2	11.0	13.5	5.2
10	32.8	16.3	16.5	15.8	18.8	8.3
25	49.4	27.4	23.4	26.0	28.4	13.9
50	59.4	37.7	30.4	36.2	36.7	19.6
100	68.5	47.9	40.1	47.6	46.5	26.5

Note: Figures are the percentage share of total income from this source accounted for by the top 5, 10, 25, 50 and 100 charities, respectively.

DOI: 10.1057/9781137522658.0006

sources, especially for legacies. For four sources of income – legacies, government, donations from individuals and internally generated income – the largest 100 organizations have just under 50 per cent of the total income from this source. Fee income appears slightly less concentrated, possibly reflecting its dispersal across large numbers of private schools operating in mainly regional contexts, rather than nationally.

Reliance on particular funding streams: 'pure' and 'impure' charities

Is reliance on a particular source of income a problem? There is a literature on financial viability or vulnerability in the nonprofit sector that generally suggests diversity to be advantageous, so that organizations do not find themselves struggling to raise funds if there is a shortfall in funding from one or another income source in any given year. However, reliance on particular sources of funding has become a matter for public debate mainly in relation to dependency on government funding.

We have already noted William Shawcross's observations. The phrase 'sock puppet' charities was coined in a report published by the Institute of Economic Affairs (IEA) (Snowdon, 2014), in reference to organizations in receipt of government funding that allegedly use that funding to lobby for more spending and government intervention in particular fields. Christopher Snowdon, the report's author, believes that this practice 'subverts democracy' and that charities engaging in lobbying government (though this is not defined clearly; what one person recognizes as the legitimate role of charities in pointing out unmet social needs is, for another, illegitimate advocacy on behalf of a producer group) in any shape or form should not receive public funding.

In similar vein, Seddon (2007) has argued that depending on the proportion of funding received by a charity that was derived from the state, the benefits of charitable status should be withdrawn. His proposals would not affect the majority of charities, since 61 per cent receive either no government funding, or such funding accounts for under 30 per cent of their income. But 14 per cent of charities receive between 30 and 70 per cent of their income from the state. Seddon suggests that these organizations could continue to receive some benefits of charitable status, and that they would be designated state-funded charities. He floated the possibility that charitable status could be withdrawn altogether from organizations that drew at least 70 per cent of their income from statutory sources. But as these organizations work disproportionately in certain

DOI: 10.1057/9781137522658.0006

areas, such as mental health, which are widely viewed as a challenging terrain for fundraisers (Body and Breeze, 2015), might this proposal, if ever implemented, trigger a spiral of decline in such organizations and render them more vulnerable to closure?

Let us suppose that we took at face value the implications of Shawcross's statement that the only 'true' charities are those that rely solely on donations from individuals, and Seddon's proposition that charitable status should be conditional on the proportion of government funding received. What would the distribution of such charities look like? We use our data to identify charities whose incomes are derived entirely from donations by individuals and fundraising, legacies, grants from non-statutory bodies, the Big Lottery Fund and their investments. In Table 2.5 we consider this by stratifying our sample charities in several ways. In the left-hand column we identify only those charities which receive no funding from either the state or from individuals paying fees. The next column refers to charities which receive no funding from government, but which do receive fees from individuals. Moving to the right, there are three columns which correspond to Seddon's propositions that the nature of charity regulation ought to change depending on the proportion of funding received from government. The rightmost column is the total number of charities in each ICNPO category, and the five main columns are percentage figures. Thus, 67 per cent of charities in the mental health field in our sample receive at least 70 per cent of their income from government. The advantage of presenting the data in this way, compared to Table 2.1, is that it shows how, even within a subsector that appears to have strong reliance on a particular income source, nevertheless there is great variability between individual organizations within subsectors of the charity population.

Depending on the column being considered, we can see that the size of the charity population varies considerably, as does the mix of activities. The 'pure' charities – those which receive neither contracts from government, nor fees from individuals – account for rather less than 18 per cent of the total number of organizations, and 11 per cent of the sector's income. They would be heavily concentrated in a small subset of the charity population. Only in the ICNPO class of grant-making foundations would we find that organizations funded entirely from private sources accounted for a majority of the funds of that subsector – which is expected in this case, as their funding derives largely from endowments. Various hospital and rehabilitation charities – many of which are NHS

TABLE 2.5   *'Pure' charities? The proportion of charities, by ICNPO, with specific funding profiles*

ICNPO	No public money, no individual fees (%)	No public money, receives fees from individuals (%)	Proportion of income from government (%)			N
			Under 30 (%)	30–70 (%)	Over 70 (%)	
Primary and secondary education	4	59	20	2	13	988
Social services	10	8	14	21	47	971
Religious congregations	27	30	29	7	7	765
Culture and arts	9	19	42	19	10	516
Grant-making foundations	72	6	11	6	4	418
Housing	11	35	13	14	28	413
International activities	37	7	23	19	13	226
Nursing homes	7	9	45	23	15	213
Hospitals and rehabilitation	45	16	18	7	14	180
Environment	18	12	28	17	25	171
Other philanthropic intermediaries	7	5	12	40	36	160
Research	29	14	22	17	18	157
Other education	6	19	21	13	41	155
Economic, social and community development.	9	8	18	27	38	149
Employment and training	8	9	14	21	48	145
Professional associations	11	25	31	23	10	143
Sport	8	18	33	24	17	139
Law and legal services	5	2	10	22	62	133
Animal protection	21	24	41	11	3	122
Income support, maintenance	43	8	30	10	9	121
Other health services	23	9	33	9	25	116
Civic and advocacy	7	10	22	23	37	115
Mental health	5	6	10	12	67	110
Medical research	47	7	33	9	5	104
Total number of organizations	1294	1526	1601	1006	1565	6,992
% of total	18.5	21.8	22.9	14.4	22.4	100
Total income (£ mn)	4831	9713	12375	5966	12452	45337
Percentage of total	10.6	21.4	27.3	13.2	27.5	

Note: Only charities with incomes greater than £500 000, and only ICNPO categories with at least 100 charities in sample, are included. Figures by ICNPO are row percentages. Highlighted cells are those which contain at least one-third of organizations in that ICNPO category.

Source: Calculated from sample data from charity accounts.

DOI: 10.1057/9781137522658.0006

charitable trust funds – and medical research charities mean that these categories of charity come closest to having a majority receiving neither public money nor individual fees.

Public funding is, on the other hand, extremely important to certain subsectors. Two-thirds of charities operating in mental health, three-fifths of those operating in law and legal services, and just under one-half of social services charities and those operating in the fields of employment and training, receive at least 70 per cent of their funding from the government. Conversely, very small proportions of organizations in these fields of activity (typically 10 per cent or lower) received no public money whatsoever. If one were to take this approach to its logical conclusion, denying the benefits of charitable status to organizations depending on their reliance on statutory sources of funding, the charitable sector would be reduced in scale and contribution substantially; and depending on the view one takes of whether state intervention crowds out voluntary contributions, the result could well be that certain types of charity would not be in a position at all to appeal for charitable support.

Are the criticisms of 'sock puppet' charities defensible? Spokespersons for the charitable sector, such as Sir Stephen Bubb of ACEVO, have noted that 'charities must be free to speak about the injustices they see on the ground, whether they are contracting with government or not'. Others, such as Neil Cleeveley of the National Association for Voluntary and Community Action (NAVCA), have linked Snowden's suggestion to the roundly condemned comments made by Eric Pickles (Conservative Secretary of State for Communities and Local Government, 2010–15) – and later repeated by the then-Charities Minister Brooks Newmark – that 'charities should stick to their knitting' – in other words, that they should be passive deliverers of service, rather overlooking the historical role of charities in campaigning for change (Burne James, 2015).

Critics of the receipt of public funding by charities should also note that contracts are awarded through open and transparent processes: should pro-voluntarists not celebrate the success of charities who receive such awards? It is also in the nature of public service contracts that they are large, as efficiency in procurement processes is likely to dictate that tenders are sought for large-scale contracts. It therefore follows that public funding is likely to account for significant proportions of the income of organizations, particularly when large-scale contracts

DOI: 10.1057/9781137522658.0006

for delivering services across geographical areas are involved. It could also be pointed out that notwithstanding their proportionate dependence on public funding, the amounts received by charities are dwarfed by payments made by government to private companies involved in service delivery contracts, in a form of corporate welfare highlighted by Farnsworth (2015).

We should note that this analysis refers only to those organizations that are in the upper end of the size distribution of registered charities – those of £500,000 income/expenditure or larger. Although this covers nine-tenths of the economic weight of the sector, only around 7 per cent of the total number of registered charities have an income greater than £500,000. The vast majority are much smaller, with a median income of around £13,000, and only a small proportion receives income from the government. If we were to look at survey data from the major national surveys of charities and other third sector organizations in England (e.g., Ipsos MORI, 2008), the picture would be very different. Most of the organizations reliant entirely on voluntary sources of income would be small, run entirely by volunteers, less likely to be dealing with problems of social exclusion and complex disadvantage, and located (as we show in the next chapter) in the most prosperous parts of the country.

Conclusions

We have shown the distribution of various sources of the incomes of registered charities across the range of charitable causes, and demonstrated the extent to which certain forms of income are concentrated in particular subsets of the charity population. We have also indicated the reliance of subsets of charities on particular funding streams.

As we have noted, discussions about the nature of charitable organizations selectively focus on the distribution of resources, either in the aggregate or for particular sources of income, in order to advance an ideological perspective. Instead of engaging in a disinterested debate about what charitable organizations can or cannot do, the focus is on whether or not organizations should receive particular funding sources, and, if so, whether they deserve charitable status. But questions about the concentration of charitable resources seem to be posed only in relation to those organizations that receive government funding. Other sources of income – notably, legacies – are even more concentrated, yet

DOI: 10.1057/9781137522658.0006

there is no suggestion of restraining the market power of those organizations that are very successful at persuading people to remember them in their wills. Receipt of government income has also been used to query whether or not organizations can be regarded as 'pure' charities, although as yet there has been no move to remove charitable privileges from such organizations.

In many ways, these discussions are about the logical outcomes of competitive market forces which, in the charitable sector, as elsewhere, tend towards concentration. We are not sure why Conservative commentators should be exercised by this; presumably the awarding of public service contracts to charitable organizations reflects a considered assessment of the quality of the work they do, and therefore the virtues of voluntarism. To the extent that it shrinks the state one might also expect them to support the placement of contracts for public services delivery with voluntary organizations. A better target for the critics' ire might be the global service companies that are sweeping the board in public service markets.

But perhaps the complaint has nothing to do with dependence on government, and much more to do with the propensity of charities to speak out and campaign, criticising the government when doing so, on matters that concern those groups in need of their services. In this regard, large, professionalized charities may be seen by the government and by conservatives as an alternative power base, to be muzzled if necessary, and its credibility undermined by critics of large salaries, government dependency and so forth. The debate is not, as it should be, about the scope and limits to voluntary initiative.

These figures also serve to highlight the challenges faced by causes that receive relatively small shares of the charitable funding cake, as well as demonstrate the difficulties facing organizations which are likely to lose substantial amounts of public funding. A loss of 10 per cent of the public funding currently received would require some subsectors of the charity population to double their current levels of fundraising income to compensate. Discussion of the distribution of income across charities has not been associated with in-depth debate about how to steer any growth in charitable fundraising to less favoured causes. We have policies about nudging (John et al., 2011), which are designed to promote more pro-social behaviours but such nudging, thus far, is about prompting individuals to consider charitable donations in general. For example, experiments through which those giving advice to people writing wills

DOI: 10.1057/9781137522658.0006

can prompt them to consider charitable donations have been shown to raise the proportions of those who make provision for a charitable legacy, rather than steering them to specific causes (Behavioural Insights Team, 2014). Whether such initiatives will do anything to level out historical disparities rather than stabilizing or even reinforcing them remains to be seen.

Note

1   Information on the total value of Lottery funding for good causes and the number of projects funded is from http://www.lotterygoodcauses.org.uk/good-causes.

DOI: 10.1057/9781137522658.0006

3

Spatial Logics: The Geographical Distribution of Charities and Charitable Resources

Abstract: *It has long been recognized that charitable activity and charitable organizations are distributed very unevenly. Recently some relatively simplistic formulations have postulated the existence of 'charity deserts', areas with few registered charitable organizations in which there is a dearth of social action. We question these analyses and attempt to refine them in various ways, which point to the broad conclusion that, appropriately specified, there are significant variations between places in the distribution of charitable resources, which appear closely related to economic conditions. The logic of charity however implies that such gaps will not close easily if at all. Ample historical evidence points to significant and persistent variations. The chapter also reviews recent policy proposals regarding what might be done about so-called charity deserts.*

Mohan, John and Beth Breeze. *The Logic of Charity: Great Expectations in Hard Times.* Basingstoke: Palgrave Macmillan, 2016. DOI: 10.1057/9781137522658.0007.

John Stuart Mill famously argued that there was a mismatch between the distribution of charitable resources and social needs. He stated, in 1848, that charity 'almost always does too much or too little: it lavishes its bounty in one place, and leaves people to starve in another' (Mill, 1848). Policy discussion in the first decades of the twenty-first century has focused on the distribution of charitable organizations, notably through the Centre for Social Justice (CSJ), a think-tank closely associated with the Conservative Party, which has repeatedly drawn attention to so-called charity deserts – places where few registered charities exist. In its initial formulation (Conservative Party, 2007), the emphasis was on the need to establish formal voluntary organizations in what were termed 'volunteering deserts'. By doing so, residents would have opportunities to volunteer, which in turn would generate social capital and strengthen communities.

In the CSJ's (2013) report 'Something's Got to Give', which argued for greater involvement of the charitable and social enterprise sectors in solving social problems, we find a re-articulation of this idea. The CSJ's argument here rests on comparisons of the distribution of charitable organizations relative to population, from around one charity per thousand residents of Blackpool to eight–or more charities per thousand in some London boroughs. This means, according to the CSJ, that large areas do not have access to the distinctive contributions that charitable organizations make to solving social problems, and that the only source of social action in such communities is the 'dysfunctional state'.

To what extent, though, is there a close match between the geographical distribution of charitable resources and the pattern of need for those resources? Would we expect such a match, given the logic of charity; and what might be done about such mismatches as exist? Is it really defensible to conclude that the only agency in such communities is the 'dysfunctional' state?

Academic commentators have pointed to good reasons for expecting an uneven distribution of charitable resources. Salamon (1987, p. 40) articulated four key weaknesses of charity: philanthropic amateurism, paternalism, particularism and insufficiency. The first two weaknesses concern the ways in which charitable services are delivered and managed, but the latter two have direct ramifications for the distribution of services. Particularism – the individualistic, idiosyncratic and taste-driven preferences of donors and charity founders – may lead to a locality being well stocked with certain types of resources which potentially

DOI: 10.1057/9781137522658.0007

duplicate one another, whilst lacking other charitable facilities and services. Donors are free to give in accordance with their own preferences and meeting social needs may not be uppermost in their minds. They may endorse causes with which they identify, donate to charitable organizations in which they have confidence or support organizations that provide desired personal benefits. All of these may well skew donations in particular ways (see Chapter 4). Furthermore, when economic conditions mean that a community does not have the capacity to sustain services through philanthropic initiative alone, this creates a situation known as 'philanthropic insufficiency'. This concept is central to the logic of charity, and in this chapter we consider some important consequences, as well as looking at possible responses.

First, however, how would we demonstrate whether or not philanthropic initiatives had reached those in need? The difficulty we have is in determining which people and communities benefit from charitable activities. Clotfelter (1992) gives a useful example of the diffuse nature of charitable benefits by observing that, while the direct and obvious beneficiaries of a project to reduce recidivism among at-risk youth might be the targeted young people and those saved from being their future victims, if the project were to be successful it would also benefit surrounding communities (reduced fear of crime), as well as taxpayers at large (reduced costs to the criminal justice system). No reliable administrative datasets, comparable with those generated through the social security system, provide information about the extent to which individuals use the services of charities, or receive benefits in cash or in kind from them.

Given the range of charitable organizations and the diverse activities through which they discharge their public benefit obligations, as well as the diffuse, indirect and latent benefits of their activities, a recent study concluded that they reach many millions of people (Glennie and Whillans-Welldrake, 2014). However, nothing can be reliably concluded from that study about the social distribution of those benefits.

An alternative, therefore, is to consider the geographical distribution of organizations and their resources. An extensive literature, primarily drawing on evidence from the USA, has demonstrated substantial variations in the distribution of non-profit organizations, both within and between American states. The most exhaustive post–Second World War enquiry into the voluntary sector in the UK, the Wolfenden Report (1978, p. 58), concluded that the soil for voluntary action was "much more fertile" in some areas than in others. We should note that this was an argument about the distribution of resources. Nothing could be concluded from the analysis as regards contextual variations in voluntary action – in other words, whether comparable individuals, living in different communities, were more or less likely to donate money or give time depending on where they lived.

Some British studies have used local listings of voluntary organizations to map spatial patterns (e.g., Fyfe and Milligan, 2003, 2004), but these sources are not representative of the entire voluntary sector (Mohan, 2012). In this chapter, we discuss a range of large-scale administrative data, noting the difficulties in accurately mapping the distribution of charitable resources, and suggesting ways in which analyses might be refined. We illustrate the unequal geographic distribution of charitable activity, noting variations in the number of charities per capita, which are further exacerbated by variations in terms of their income sources and core purpose. We demonstrate that, broadly speaking, there are significant social gradients in the distribution of charitable organizations and their resources between communities, such that poorer communities host fewer charitable organizations and those that exist in such neighbourhoods rely more on statutory than voluntary income. We then interpret these patterns in relation to our central concern of the logic of charity, exploring implications and potential political responses.

Challenges of and approaches to mapping charitable resources

A basic analysis of the Register of Charities points to clear and significant variations in the distribution of charitable organizations. A total of 140,000 active charities were identified in England in 2011 ('active' being defined as having made at least one non-zero financial return to the Charity Commission in a five-year period), which equates to an average of around 2.5 charities per thousand people.[1] However, when this ratio is calculated for each local authority (LA), the ratio of charities to population varies by a factor of nearly 10, even discounting the outlier of the City of London, which has several hundred registered charities but a population of only 7,000; many charities are registered through solicitor's offices, which are numerous in the city.

DOI: 10.1057/9781137522658.0007

The local authorities with the most charities per thousand population were Westminster (14), Camden (8), Islington, Barnet and Hackney (all with 5). At the other end of the spectrum, Wigan, Knowsley, South Tyneside and Blackpool all had fewer than 1 charity per thousand population. Leaving aside the City of London, there is a strong negative correlation between these rates and the index of deprivation for the 148 local authorities in England in this analysis (-0.38), meaning that poorer areas have fewer charities. Does this suggest that the explanation for 'charity deserts' lies with varying levels of deprivation or prosperity?

Correlation is not causality, of course, and while these figures suggest strong associations with material conditions, mapping the geographic distribution of charitable resources is not a straightforward task. On registration with the Charity Commission, an organization must provide a main contact address and they may (but are not required to) specify their geographic area of benefit (AOB). On their annual returns they are also asked to supply information about their 'area of operation'. The information derived in this way can in principle be used to work out which charities are operating where, but it can also be challenging for three main reasons: the 'headquarters effect', obsolescence and imprecision.

Headquarters effect

If we simply use the addresses of charity administrative offices to assess the distribution of charitable expenditures, we will overestimate expenditure and activity in regions or local authorities that have significant numbers of charity headquarters. This HQ effect is exemplified by the National Trust, whose main office is located in Swindon, but no one would suggest that we allocate all of its £400 million annual expenditure to that local authority. At least 60 per cent of charities with incomes greater than £1 million have a head office with branches in other regions. Thirty-five per cent of such charities were in London, whereas its share of the charity population as a whole was barely half that (18 per cent). Regional studies of voluntary action have also identified projects run by large national organizations based in London (Mohan et al., 2011).

It is possible to disaggregate charity expenditures by using a government dataset, formerly known as the Interdepartmental Business Register (IDBR) (now the Business Structure Database). This was used by Kane and Clark (2009) to reapportion charitable expenditures between regions in proportion to employment at the branches of national organizations.

DOI: 10.1057/9781137522658.0007

For the £31 billion of expenditure by the organizations considered in their study, it was estimated that nearly £1.9 billion was spent overseas. Nearly half of the £13 billion of expenditure of charities based in London was redistributed elsewhere in the UK, with only a small inflow (relatively speaking) of £500 million from outside London. Expenditure totalling £1.25 billion was reapportioned from the charities of south-east England, but this was balanced by an almost equal inflow from elsewhere. The biggest beneficiaries of this redistribution were north-east England and the East Midlands, gaining around 50 per cent when aggregate expenditures were compared with the total for charities based in those regions. Even so, per capita expenditures remained relatively high in London compared to the rest of England and Wales – more than 50 per cent higher than the next regions, South East and South West England. Thus, the allowances made for branch structures of large registered charities do something to reduce disparities in charitable expenditures but by no means remove them.

Obsolescence

As many charities have long histories, their 'area of benefit' may become historically obsolete if it were defined in relation to an administrative unit that existed at the time the charity was founded, but has now ceased to exist. Table 3.1 gives examples of types of obsolete administrative units

TABLE 3.1   *Area of benefit types, number of charities and expenditures*

Area of benefit	Mean expenditure	Median expenditure	99th percentile	Total expenditure £m	Number of charities
Ancient parish	17231	1352	265968	23	1,692
London Borough	343563	64716	4331413	515	1,994
Urban district/rural district	37215	3623	525759	17	584
Parish	13870	3254	155381	171	14,853
Total				727	19,123

Note: Type of area of benefit is based on presence or absence of terms (e.g., 'ancient parish') in the text descriptions of administrative units provided by charities.

Source: Register of Charities.

DOI: 10.1057/9781137522658.0007

that are still used by almost 20,000 charities with a combined annual expenditure (averaged over the 2007–11 period) of £727 million.

Ancient parishes were formally abolished in 1851, but some 1,700 registered general charities have areas of benefit defined in relation to such entities. Other illustrations would be urban or rural districts, and county or municipal boroughs, which were abolished at various dates (principally 1965, for some London boroughs, and 1974, in the case of boroughs outside London, and urban and rural districts). Several hundred charities, spending around £17 million, still exist that are defined in terms of those extinct units.

While the great majority of charities defined in terms of obsolete administrative units or in terms of parishes are very small in terms of income, over 300 have mean annual expenditures greater than £100,000. Several established parochial charities in central London have expenditures above £1 million. A charity associated with one former parish in an inner London borough serves an area that now has a population of some 9,000 people, but spends in excess of £1 million per annum on the residents of that area, primarily in the form of social services oriented towards elderly people. This has the effect of raising per capita social services expenditure in that locality by some 30 per cent compared to the rest of the borough. It is reasonable to suppose that the composition of the population, and the needs to be met there, have changed considerably since it was established, and it is a noteworthy feature of charity that access to its benefits can depend on historical accidents of this kind.

Imprecision

Charities may, but are not required to, specify an area of benefit, although more than half leave this undefined. Charities are not obliged to provide benefit equally across their AOB: they may concentrate their efforts on a subset of locations, but in some circumstances they can have a very wide remit indeed. The Royal National Lifeboat Institution (RNLI) mounts rescue services within 100 miles of the entire coastline of Great Britain which, for historical reasons, includes the Republic of Ireland. Even relatively small organizations can have considerable reach, such as the Mountain Bothies Association, a Scottish charity with a turnover of around £100,000 a year, which repairs and maintains old buildings in remote rural areas as basic shelters for outdoor pursuits enthusiasts, and does so from Cape Wrath in the north of Scotland to the Welsh Brecon

DOI: 10.1057/9781137522658.0007

Beacons. Conversely many small charities, such as Parent-Teacher Associations, established to support particular schools, have an area of benefit defined as the 'catchment area of the school' – which, as many parents will testify, can be a very small area indeed.

If areas of benefit do not provide a complete answer, what other information is available? The Charity Commission now gathers information about the 'area of operation'. Charities are asked to report the names of the local authorities in which their activities take place; they can identify a single authority, between two and ten (in which case they are requested to name them), a 'wide' area of operation (greater than ten local authorities, not named), 'England and Wales and international' and 'international only'. Using this information, and combining it with ancillary information about charities' areas of benefit, we assess which charities have what kind of geographical reach, as summarized in Table 3.2. Around three-fifths of all charities operate within one local authority, but they are relatively small, as can be seen from the mean and median expenditures, which rise steadily as the scale of operation increases – the mean, which of course is heavily influenced by very large charities, rises from £83,000 for local-authority level charities to over £1.1 million for national and international organizations. The median for local authority-level charities is, at under £10,000, well below that of the median for the entire charity population. It may be surprising that the mean and median for those charities operating solely at the international scale are lower than for the 'national/international' category, but there are a large number of small charities, operating through close community links with overseas partners (e.g., parish-to-parish connections within faith communities) which partly explain this.

TABLE 3.2   *Area of operation of charities: numbers, mean and median expenditure*

Scale of operation	Number	%	Mean expenditure (£)	Median expenditure (£)
Within one local authority	87,971	62.2	83113	9778
2–10 named local authorities	20,109	14.2	256794	20384
'Wide' area; more than 10 local authorities	18,678	13.2	489050	25666
England, Wales and international	11,479	8.1	1117503	34793
International only	3,305	2.3	345485	17846

Note: Includes all charities on register reporting at least one non-zero expenditure return, 2007–11.
Source: Register of Charities.

DOI: 10.1057/9781137522658.0007

Of those charities operating within a single local authority, some 40 per cent of these were accounted for by the following types of organization, according to the ICNPO classification: economic, social and community development (7,600; this is a broad category which will include several thousand women's institutes as well as community centres); parent-teacher associations (9,800); playgroups (5,800); uniformed groups (Scouts, Guides, Cubs and so on; 4,800); village halls (4,800); and sports and recreational groups (5000). These are typically small and account for limited proportions of total charitable activity, at least if we take recorded expenditure as a guide.

Another way to assess the distribution of charitable resources would be to use this information to generate estimates of the level of charitable expenditure in any given geographical area. However, the types of organizations for which this is feasible tend to be relatively small. The vast majority (at least four out of five) of the groups named here operate within a single local authority but their expenditures are quite low. In contrast, fields such as social services are characterized by a very different size distribution of organizations. We can allocate approximately 35 per cent of total charitable expenditures to named local authorities; the remainder is spent by organizations that operate across at least ten local authorities or on a national or international basis, so we are unable to specify precisely where spending and activity take place. So returning to the analysis of the numbers of charitable organizations, if we only consider charities who say they operate within one local authority, thereby making some allowance for headquarters effects (discussed later), the strength of the association with the Index of Material Deprivation (IMD) rises to −0.56; this is unlikely to be a chance result, and it does suggest strong associations between the distribution of charities and variations in socioeconomic conditions between local authority areas.

In short, analyses of local authority-level variations in charity: population ratios suggest a strong and significant negative association with deprivation, which strengthens when allowance is made only for those organizations that operate within one local authority. But there are limits to how far it is possible to use administrative information to identify more closely the communities in which charities spend their money, because the charitable organizations which can be linked to specific geographical areas are generally small. A refinement would be to choose particular subsets of organizations, and then analyze variations in their resources across communities. Examples of this are given in Mohan

DOI: 10.1057/9781137522658.0007

(2015), in which comparisons are drawn between organizations such as PTAs and hospices; in the case of the former, private support to schools through such vehicles varies in a way that demonstrates strong associations with levels of deprivation in the community. As an alternative to a focus on specific causes, another analytical possibility is to use survey data to look at neighbourhood-level charities.

Neighbourhood charities: distribution, resources and relationships

The National Survey of Third Sector Organizations (NSTSO), a large-scale survey conducted in England during 2008, allows us to generate a more accurate map of the geographical spread of charitable organizations, and to gain an understanding of the populations they serve and their different sources of income. This survey included over 40,000 responses from registered charities providing information that enabled us to distinguish between those operating at the neighbourhood scale, or operating within local authorities, from those operating at a larger, national or international, scale.

Furthermore, detailed geographical disaggregation was possible, since local authorities were named, and banded information was provided on the level of deprivation of the immediate locality of the respondent's address. Such data can be cross-referenced to population statistics, allowing estimation of how many people live within areas characterized by particular levels of deprivation within each region, and therefore estimation of ratios of organizations to population. The obvious precedent is the work of Clifford (2012) on neighbourhood-level voluntary organizations, which has analyzed the same survey data for the population of third sector organizations. Our focus is narrower – only registered charities are considered – but we take a different approach to the identification and classification of neighbourhood organizations, and go into greater detail as regards their characteristics and activities.

The ability of the survey to capture data on small registered charities operating at the neighbourhood scale is pertinent given Deakin's (2001) suggestion that the study of civil society and voluntary action requires a 'new respect for the local', and given the post-2010 emphasis in public policy on the significance of neighbourhoods as bases for social action. While the rhetoric of the 'Big Society' is no longer as salient as it was

DOI: 10.1057/9781137522658.0007

during the 2010 general election, there is no doubt that the neighbourhood is seen as an important element of Conservative policy, and that
neighbourhood-based social action has been valued at the highest level
(Ware, 2012). This survey therefore gives us an opportunity to consider
the potential (and also potential limitations) of such action.

The NSTSO is the largest survey ever undertaken of voluntary
organizations in one country; the background and methodology are
fully explained by Ipsos MORI (2008). The dataset enables us to focus
solely on charities operating on a neighbourhood scale – those directly
impacting on local quality of life, as opposed to those that happen to be
based in a particular location but which have a wider (or alternative)
field of operation and impact (such as head offices of national or regional
charities). Here we review findings on the geographical distribution of
neighbourhood charities; the type of activities they undertake; their
beneficiaries; the extent of volunteerism; their funding sources; and their
concerns about resource scarcity.

Scale of operation of neighbourhood charities by legal form

We begin by looking at a breakdown of scale of operation by legal form.
This includes other third sector legal forms for comparison (Table 3.3) –
one reason for this being that there are other legal forms of third sector
organization through which social action takes place in communities.

Registered charities take one of two legal forms: unincorporated
charities or charitable companies. Unincorporated charities account for
64 per cent of responses to the survey and represent 78 per cent of neighbourhood-level organizations; conversely, incorporated charities (13 per
cent of respondents), which of course tend to be larger, account for a
much larger proportion of the organizations operating at the regional or
national scale (18 and 15 per cent, respectively), while they only account
for 3.5 per cent of neighbourhood-scale organizations. Unincorporated
associations have limitations on what they are able to do (Morris, 2012).
They do not have a legal personality that is entirely distinct from their
trustees, they cannot own property in their own right and they cannot
make contracts, including contracts of employment. An important aim
of policy in the governments led by the Prime Minister, David Cameron,
has been to open up greater scope for voluntary organizations to deliver
public services. But many neighbourhood charities may not wish to do
this, and the preponderance of unincorporated associations among them

DOI: 10.1057/9781137522658.0007

TABLE 3.3 *Legal form of third-sector organization by scale of operation*

	Scale of operation										
	Neighbourhood		Within local authority		Regional		National/ international			Total	
Organization type	N	Col. %	N	Col. %	N	Col. %	N	Col. %	Total (N)	Total (Col. %)
Incorporated charities	1,121	3.5	6,627	13.3	5,137	17.9	8,646	15.1	21,531	12.9
Unincorporated charities	24,811	78.0	32,769	65.7	14,550	50.8	34,170	59.9	106,301	63.5
Co. Ltd by Guarantee	3,389	11.0	6,811	13.7	6,843	23.9	12,251	21.5	29,295	17.5
Community Interest Co.	61	0.2	332	0.7	411	1.4	458	0.8	1,262	0.8
Ind. & Provident Soc.	2,440	7.8	3,347	6.7	1,717	6.0	1,562	2.7	9,066	5.4
Total	31,822		49,886		28,659		57,088		167,454	

Note: Authors' calculations based on data from 2008 National Survey of Third Sector Organisations.

Source: Ipsos MORI (2008).

DOI: 10.1057/9781137522658.0007

means that most are unlikely to be able to do so anyway. The government's ambitions to hand over public services to charitable organizations may therefore be only partially fulfilled. The data also show that a relatively small proportion (about 22 per cent) of neighbourhood organizations take other legal forms of non-profit action (Company Limited by Guarantee; Community Interest Company; Industrial and Provident Society), implying that if we are concerned about the scope for local action, our primary focus should be on registered charities.

Figure 3.1 cross-references scale against income for charities, examining incorporated and unincorporated charities separately. Typically, and unsurprisingly, some 56 per cent of organizations with incomes below £10,000 say that they operate at the neighbourhood or 'within local authority' scales, and the great majority of these are unincorporated associations. If this proportion applied to the charity population as a whole, it would equate to some 40,000 charities. By contrast, for the larger organizations – defined here as incomes greater than £100,000, or charities in the top 20 per cent of the size distribution – the proportion drops to below 40 per cent, and generally less than 10 per cent of organizations

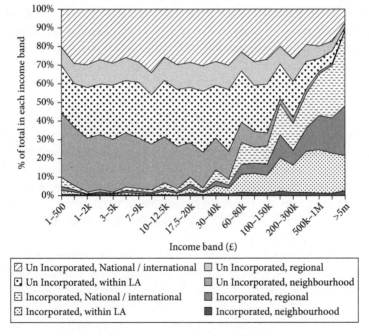

FIGURE 3.1   *Size distribution of charities by scale and legal form*

DOI: 10.1057/9781137522658.0007

of this size operate only at the neighbourhood level. Around seven-eighths of charities that claim to operate at the neighbourhood scale have incomes of less than £25,000. It is only at the upper end of the income distribution that incorporated charities, regardless of scale, account for the majority of observations, and of course relatively few charities have substantial incomes – in this survey, around 20 per cent of charities responding had incomes of £100,000 or more. So considered purely in terms of numbers of organizations, the charity population of England is dominated by small entities, the majority of which say they operate at the neighbourhood scale or, failing that, within their local authority.

Geographic spread of neighbourhood charities

We began this chapter with discussions of data on the number of all registered charities per local authority. Here we consider the geographic distribution of just those charities that operate at the neighbourhood scale. The findings, summarized in Table 3.4, show a substantial range between regions in terms of the prevalence of charitable organizations operating only at the neighbourhood scale. The highest figure estimated is in part of the South West with a regional average of just over 2 organizations per thousand population, while in the North East the corresponding figure is 0.9 organizations per thousand population. Variations within regions are much greater. The estimates are arranged by level of deprivation in the immediate locality, and the main substantive point is the contrast between the most prosperous areas, in the upper three rows of the table, and the most disadvantaged. Typically areas with an IMD of less than 15, which places them in the 25 per cent most prosperous communities, will have two to three times as many neighbourhood-level charities as areas with an IMD above 45. Thus there is a range between communities of around a factor of 6 in the numbers of charities that operate at the neighbourhood scale in different parts of England, between c.2.4 organizations per thousand population in parts of the South West, compared to around 0.4 per thousand population in areas of North West and North East England.

Although the general picture is of a gradient between the most prosperous and the most disadvantaged areas, some locations provide exceptions to the rule. But the overall picture is clear: if we consider only those charities that operate at the neighbourhood scale, there are very considerable differences in the capacities of the registered charity sector,

DOI: 10.1057/9781137522658.0007

TABLE 3.4 *Ratio of neighbourhood-level charities in England to population by region and level of deprivation*

IMD	East Midlands	East of England	London	North East	North West	South East	South West	West Midlands	Yorks and Humber
0–4.99	1.54	**1.91**	1.63	1.14	1.39	**1.96**	**1.85**	1.54	1.55
5–9.99	**1.87**	**1.99**	1.13	1.03	1.42	1.8	**1.98**	1.59	1.48
10–14.99	1.81	**1.96**	0.97	1.03	1.48	**1.86**	**2.41**	1.76	1.49
15–19.99	1.38	1.51	0.81	1.35	0.89	1.24	**2.06**	1.48	1.16
20–24.99	1.2	1.23	0.82	0.83	**0.65**	0.99	**2.1**	**0.76**	**0.73**
25–29.99	0.7	0.89	**0.76**	**0.64**	**0.54**	1.04	1.22	**0.63**	**0.77**
30–34.99	**0.73**	**0.68**	**0.71**	**0.54**	0.57	0.9	1.03	0.83	**0.52**
35–39.99	**0.71**	0.84	**0.71**	**0.44**	**0.41**	1.15	0.81	**0.65**	**0.54**
40–44.99	**0.68**	1.32	0.84	**0.64**	**0.47**	**0.69**	0.89	**0.46**	**0.36**
45–49.99	0.89	1.59	**0.73**	**0.58**	**0.66**	0.93	1.29	**0.56**	**0.53**
50–54.99	0.95	1.17	0.86	**0.59**	**0.59**	1.28	1.36	**0.71**	0.87
55+	**0.79**	1.48	1.08	0.82	0.73	1.21	1.11	**0.61**	0.87

Note: IMD = Index of Material Deprivation, ranked from least (0 – 4.99) to most deprived. Figures are numbers of organizations per 1,000 population. Highlighted figures are at least one standard deviation above or below the national average.

Source: Author's calculations from 2008 National Survey of Third Sector Organisations.

not only between regions but within them. In most regions the ratio of locally oriented organizations relative to population varies by a factor of at least 2.5. Although the correlation with disadvantage is not a perfect one there are generally around twice as many such organizations in the least deprived areas compared to the most disadvantaged ones.

Activities of neighbourhood charities

The activities undertaken by neighbourhood charities are summarized in Figure 3.2. Over 40 per cent of such organizations indicated that their primary purpose is either education and lifelong learning, or culture and leisure (the latter includes arts, music, sport and recreation). Some 9 per cent of organizations indicated that they worked in health and well-being, while a further 9 per cent regard their primary purpose as being concerned with community development and mutual aid. For other categories, frequencies were typically below 5 per cent.

Compared with their neighbourhood-scale counterparts, charities not working at the neighbourhood exhibit lower proportions working in education, lifelong learning, cultural and leisure activities, and higher

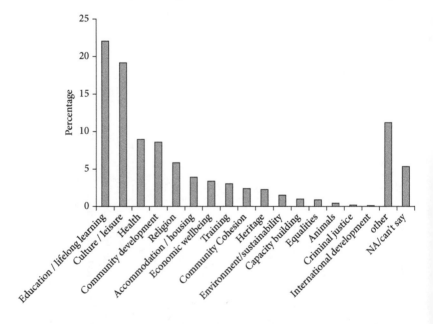

FIGURE 3.2   *Principal purposes of charities identifying themselves as 'neighbourhood-scale' organizations*

DOI: 10.1057/9781137522658.0007

proportions operating in the fields of health and religion and faith-based charity. We therefore conclude that there is a strong preponderance of 'nice to have', not 'need to have' organizations operating as neighbourhood-level charities. This is highly relevant if one is considering the potential of neighbourhood-level organizations to take on responsibilities that have been shed by the state.

Under 25 per cent of neighbourhood charitable organizations identify themselves as working primarily with people experiencing personal or social disadvantages, and a further 11 per cent identify themselves as faith-based organizations or a general 'other' category. In short, and in relation to the redistributive effects of charitable giving, many of these groups are recycling resources within relatively prosperous communities, rather than having substantial redistributive effects. This echoes findings in other qualitative studies (Odendahl, 1990; Ostrower, 1995), not to mention a long-established quantitative literature from the USA, demonstrating significant inter- and intra-urban variations at the metropolitan level in the provision of organizations contributing to quality of life in the broadest sense (Wolpert, 1988).

The voluntary nature of neighbourhood charities

Theories of philanthropic insufficiency suggest that we would find a much greater reliance upon both voluntary financial support and volunteer input in the most prosperous areas, compared to the more disadvantaged regions. We devised a four-fold classification of organizations in terms of whether or not they receive public money of any kind, and in terms of whether or not they have employees.

As shown in Table 3.5, almost exactly half of all neighbourhood charities (some 31,000) can be described as entirely voluntary in character because they have no paid staff and receive no funding from the public sector. A breakdown by level of deprivation in the immediate locality shows that half of the population of neighbourhood charities that are

TABLE 3.5 *Characteristics of neighbourhood charities: employees and receipt of public funding*

	Do not receive public money	Receive public money
Do not have employees	31,400	11,500
Have employees	4,800	15,500

DOI: 10.1057/9781137522658.0007

entirely voluntary in this sense are predominantly concentrated in the most prosperous areas of the country. By contrast, in the three most deprived areas by level of the Index of Multiple Deprivation (IMD) – areas containing some 10 per cent of England's population – we find only about 1.5 per cent of such entirely voluntary organizations.

Table 3.4 suggests that variations between rich and poor neighbourhoods are reduced to a small degree by an increase in the numbers of organizations in the most deprived areas. This is a consequence of the presence there of charities that have both statutory funding and employees. Thinking back to our theme of whether charity can step in when the state withdraws, such organizations are also heavily reliant on public funding. In the most prosperous neighbourhoods, we find that only one-third or fewer of neighbourhood charities receive any public funding, and they are therefore far less likely to be exposed to austerity measures (see also Clifford et al., 2013).

Funding: sources and concerns

The NSTSO data includes information on eight sources of funding: (1) voluntary income, including fundraising and donations; membership fees and subscriptions; grants from non-statutory bodies (principally charitable trusts, foundations and companies); and National Lottery distributors; (2) statutory income, including grants and core funding; income from contracts; (3) earned income from trading activities, including retail income, and income from investments. For neighbourhood organizations, by far the most significant sources of funding are from donations, fundraising and membership fees, named by three-quarters of organizations in total, and five-sixths of unincorporated neighbourhood charities. For incorporated charities operating at the neighbourhood scale, some 40 per cent of organizations declared voluntary income to be the most important source, but earned income was the second most important, at 16 per cent.

Statutory funding was deemed much more significant by incorporated charities operating at the within local authority scale: over 60 per cent of such charities identified statutory funding as their most important. We can also identify organizations that relied entirely upon voluntary sources of funding, and again these are heavily concentrated in the most prosperous neighbourhoods: 60 per cent are located in areas with an index of deprivation of 15 or under, which places them in the 25 per cent most prosperous areas.

DOI: 10.1057/9781137522658.0007

We can also consider organizations' own beliefs about the adequacy of their funding. They were asked about the degree of confidence they had in the level of financial resources, their ability to recruit volunteers, and the level of their financial reserves. Controlling in a logistic regression (details not shown here) for size (income), legal form, geographical scale and the principal beneficiary group, we found that local neighbourhood-level unincorporated charities, working with the general population (as opposed to targeting specific groups in need) were most optimistic about the availability of resources of various kinds. Organizations relying only on voluntary sources of income were much more confident than their counterparts receiving public money about their likely future prospects. Confidence about resources declined steadily the more disadvantaged the area.

We should note that this survey was undertaken in 2008 – in other words, before the reductions in public funding set in train by the 2010 Comprehensive Spending Review. These findings imply that it is neighbourhood organizations in prosperous communities, and not reliant upon public money, that appear best placed to ride the storm of austerity.

This evidence shows that neighbourhood charities are concentrated in the most prosperous parts of the country where they are much more likely to be entirely voluntary in character and to regard voluntary sources of income as being of greatest importance to them. In contrast we find that poorer areas have a lower proportion of neighbourhood charities per head of population, and those charitable organizations that are located in such areas are more likely to be reliant on statutory income. These quantitative findings are echoed by complementary work that intensively studied the charitable 'ecology' in two areas within one local authority (Lindsey, 2013). The findings pointed to relatively strong and integrated networks of local charities relying solely on voluntary effort and charitable fundraising in the prosperous parts of the suburbs, in contrast to the dependence on external public funding of the small number of relatively large charities which constituted the charitable landscape of a proximate, but very disadvantaged community (Lindsey, 2013). The same study suggests that charities in the more prosperous parts of the community enrich the social and cultural life of their neighbourhood. By contrast, staff and volunteers associated with charities and community groups in the more disadvantaged area consistently reported the impact of material deprivation on their ability both to raise funds and to recruit

DOI: 10.1057/9781137522658.0007

volunteers. On the face of it these analyses appear to support the notion of charity deserts, but we would place a rather different interpretation on the evidence than that of the Centre for Social Justice (2013).

The CSJ, charity deserts and policy

In our judgement, there are clear weaknesses inherent in an analysis that focuses, as the CSJ does, only on ratios of charitable organizations to population without at least beginning to question whether such ratios provided meaningful insight into exactly where charitable activity was taking place. We sought to refine the analysis by using information that allowed a better specification of which charitable organizations were active in which geographical areas (charities operating within individual local authorities, or saying that they operated at the 'neighbourhood geographical scale'). Clearly, the patterns of variation in the distribution of charitable organizations and their activities persist when the analysis is refined to focus on neighbourhood charities. We also demonstrate the very strong correlations between levels of deprivation in local authorities and the distribution of registered charities operating at the within-local authority scale, and very strong socio-economic gradients in the distribution of organizations which operate at the neighbourhood scale. These results are more defensible than the CSJ's findings insofar as efforts have been made to consider only those organizations which can be linked directly to particular communities.

The CSJ's emphasis upon registered charities also constitutes a partial approach to the mapping of social initiatives. There are other forms of social action: some third sector organizations take legal forms that are not charitable. However, numerically, registered charities constitute the largest element of the voluntary sector, and the numbers of other regulated non-profits exhibit similar socio-economic gradients. This is certainly the case looking at the large national surveys of third sector organizations in England for 2008 and 2010 (Clifford, 2012).

A further riposte to the CSJ's argument might be to point to the presence of grassroots voluntary organizations that operate below the regulatory radar. The complexities of mapping such groups in a systematic manner mean that it is difficult to generalize about their distribution, but an argument can be made that the pattern of charities is in part a function of the distribution of people who are comfortable with the bureaucratic formalities of registering and running a charity. From this perspective it is plausible that so-called charity deserts contain other forms of social action since groups operating in more prosperous neighbourhoods may be more likely to be able to call on the support of educated individuals to ensure that charity registration is carried out.

The emphasis solely on the distribution of all types of charities also ignores the roles that statutory bodies may play in supporting voluntarism. This might take the form of provision of premises through which unregistered groups could come together, or in-kind support by public sector personnel. Far from squeezing out voluntary initiative, statutory bodies can actively underpin it.

The focus of the CSJ reports on registered charities alone is therefore partial. The same can be said of their neglect of the possibility that social gradients in the distribution of organizations might be explained by, or even associated with, material circumstances. Such circumstances are not mentioned in the CSJ's report, which largely ignores the burdens (unemployment, ill-health, caring responsibilities) carried by people in disadvantaged communities, which make them less likely to engage. Nor do the CSJ reports mention the large-scale social challenges being dealt with by statutory bodies in those more deprived areas. Further, the 'charity deserts' argument suggests that the problems of disadvantaged areas are related to their failure to found enough charitable organizations to cope with the challenges that they face, rather than being due to deeper structural issues.

But whether anything can, or ought, to be done about variations in the geographic distribution of charities is an important question. We might begin by asking about the basis for our expectations about the distribution of resources, and at what point do variations become problems? There is an expectation that the state will do a broadly equitable job of allocating public funds, but given what we know about how donors take decisions, would it be reasonable to expect a close match between the distribution of charitable resources and dimensions of need? Social policy often uses the language of justice to consider the pattern of resources – for example, territorial justice would describe a situation in which the distribution of resources was proportionate to the relative needs of different communities. Is this appropriate in the context of a large and heterogeneous voluntary sector? We have used small area indicators of deprivation as a basis for mapping the distribution of registered charities working at the neighbourhood scale. We know there are steep gradients between neighbourhoods. But if charitable activity is an expression of individual and/or community preference, is there any basis at all for making judgements about resource distributions? Who is entitled to determine the causes to be supported by a donor, and on what grounds?

For some, of course, the language of territorial or any other form of social justice is not appropriate, and these variations are not a problem. Some commentators would argue that such patterns are the natural outcomes of a social order in which communities are free to generate and support their institutions (or not, as the case may be). David Green (1993, p. 21) once argued that welfare systems need to 'take the risk of under-government' – in other words, there may be unmet needs, and variations between communities in the provision of voluntary resources, but these are tolerable, and defensible. From Green's perspective, it is more important to prioritize localism and voluntary initiative than it is to impose equality from above. Indeed, some have disputed the notion of philanthropic insufficiency altogether, contending that voluntary action can deliver comprehensive services. According to Arthur Seldon (1990, p. 250), after the Second World War the British state simply 'mounted the already-galloping horse' of voluntary initiative. Had that not happened, presumably voluntary organizations would have continued to spread and universalize their benefits. These authors were clearly prioritizing community control and initiative over comprehensiveness and equity; the voluntary hospital system delivered its benefits very unevenly (Mohan, 2003).

An alternative perspective would see the pattern of distribution and funding of charitable organizations as an expression of competition for resources, in which some organizations and communities are more successful than others. This is a competitive market, and so on what basis can we judge the outcome? Why would it inherently be a problem if there was a concentration of resources, as indeed there is, in large national charities (Backus and Clifford, 2013), if this simply reflected the relative efficiency and popularity of the organizations concerned?

If, on the other hand, charitable funding undermines or runs counter to the pattern of funding for democratically mandated goals – such as the equalization of educational opportunities – then there might be circumstances in which inequality constituted a problem. For example, a study of private philanthropic support for school boards in the USA demonstrates that the larger sums raised by schools serving more prosperous communities serve to embed and enhance processes of socio-economic

DOI: 10.1057/9781137522658.0007

segregation, as well as potentially subverting political processes when wealthier donors are willing to pay to promote preferred versions of school reform (Reich, 2006). In the UK, we have witnessed occasions where philanthropic support has been claimed to be interfering with public policy goals, for example, when support from major donors for hospital facilities became an issue in the planned rationalization of London's hospital services (Mohan and Gorsky, 2001).

Conclusions: the political implications of mapping charitable resources

How does the unequal distribution of charitable resources relate to wider political action and strategies? A key feature of the governments led by David Cameron is an attempt to differentiate the present Conservatives from their Thatcherite predecessors. According to Alan Ware (2012), the Thatcher governments were distinctive for their attack on intermediate institutions standing between individuals and global economic and political forces. Cameron wanted a strategy that would reassure the electorate there were community-level institutions, providing a strong local infrastructure for community engagement. In this vision, the process of providing public goods is best devolved to local communities; localism is celebrated. The focus on neighbourhoods, and social action at the local level, is therefore a strong feature of current policy, to which there are several strands, whether or not we refer to them under the generic umbrella of the 'Big Society'. But whether current policy initiatives would achieve a better match between the distribution of needs and the distribution of charitable organizations must be open to question.

There have been some initiatives designed to shift resources, including place-based philanthropic initiatives such as community foundations, which have benefited from a number of government-matched funding schemes to encourage philanthropists to support causes and social action projects in their community. But finding private donors to match government funding is likely to prove more difficult to find in areas of disadvantage: for example, Wales has historically had fewer 'million pound donors' than other regions of the UK (Breeze, 2012, p. 10). Thus far, the resources generated by community foundations are typically £4–£5 per head of population, contrasting with the c.£250 per head that will be withdrawn from some communities in anticipated public funding

DOI: 10.1057/9781137522658.0007

cuts. While these foundations are certainly focussed on local community needs, this indicates the scale of the challenge to be faced.

There are at least three other political strategies currently being pursued by the Conservative government elected in 2015. Firstly, as noted in the previous chapter, there are attempts to understand and create behavioural change, popularly known as 'nudging' in charitable giving. Secondly, in the context of a wider transfer of power from central to local government, communities are given the possibility of setting up and running their own services. Thirdly, the development of mutuals, cooperatives and social enterprises has been encouraged, by spinning out elements of the public sector into non-profit organizations, and opening up much larger segments of public services provision to competition.

Whether these policies on their own can do much about the distribution of voluntary resources is debatable: the sums available from government have largely been for pilot projects, rather than for long-term funding. The general tenor of these proposed solutions involves a return to small-scale community-based social action, to be encouraged by some deregulation of provisions in public service contracting and the formation of new social enterprises. But such initiatives are unlikely to even up variations between communities in the resources available to them. While David Cameron has referred to the ways in which charities bring communities together,[2] the reality is one of strong networks of neighbourhood-level charities in the most prosperous communities, largely insulated from risks of withdrawal of public funding. There is a need for consideration of how donors and supporters of charities might be persuaded to direct funding to areas of disadvantage. But whether this is realistic requires that we turn, in the next chapter, to a discussion of the logic of charity from the perspective of private, individual donors.

Notes

1   This is a lower figure than reported in Chapter 1; the Commission's Annual Reports include subsidiaries of charities and do not identify 'active' ones in the manner described here, but the historic statistics cannot be disaggregated.

2   https://www.gov.uk/government/news/new-law-to-protect-vulnerable-from-rogue-fundraisers

4

The Supply of Philanthropy in Relation to Beneficiary Demand

Abstract: *This chapter presents a body of qualitative data to explore the complex processes of philanthropic decision-making. Donor autonomy, and the historically typical dominance of 'taste-based' giving, generates a heterogeneous charity population that is not, on the whole, concerned with matching resources with needs: charity therefore falls short of political expectations. The institutional logic of philanthropy is characterized as supply-led and influenced by three factors: identification with the cause; confidence in the charitable organization being funded; and desire for personal enrichment alongside doing good. This contrasts sharply with the rule-governed allocation of resources by state agencies according to democratically-agreed preferences. Therefore the distribution of philanthropic resources will not easily change in response to new political priorities, and will not necessarily match the pattern of social need.*

Mohan, John and Beth Breeze. *The Logic of Charity: Great Expectations in Hard Times.* Basingstoke: Palgrave Macmillan, 2016. DOI: 10.1057/9781137522658.0008.

To what extent can charitable activity result in a proportionate matching of the distribution of resources with the pattern of social needs? In a context of austerity, as in contemporary Britain, can we anticipate that there will be an increase in private donations to compensate for the withdrawal of the state, and if so will those contributions be well-targeted? Is it likely that donations of charitable resources will flow to causes and communities most in need of them?

We argue that the logic of charity means that it is unlikely that charitable efforts will match resources with needs, and that it will therefore fall short of the expectations of politicians. There are three reasons for this:

1   'Meeting need' is not a central concern of most charities, and individual donors have a range of motives for giving, not all of which are associated with allocating resources to areas of need.
2   Philanthropic decision-making is complex and largely immune to political influence, so we are unlikely to see a shift in the priorities of donors as the state is rolled back.
3   Donors value their autonomy and the freedom of giving, which they contrast favourably with the compulsory nature of taxation. Hence the causes they choose to support may, or may not, be aligned with wider social priorities and the political programmes of the government in power.

As we have shown in Chapter 1, only a small percentage of charities serve those in need as a primary client group. The range of potential charitable causes is considerable, and in practice 'need' will often be secondary to other criteria such as excellence (in the case of sport or the arts), universal reach (in the case of human rights or medical research) or particularism (helping people belonging to a specific sub-group – e.g., young people, or those with a specific medical condition – or protecting the environment in a specific geographical area – e.g., a wildlife trust).

People tend to be surprised that being 'for charity' does not equate with being 'pro-poor'. Indeed, previous UK research found a broad public consensus that 'to be a charitable concern, a recipient had to be "in need"' (Fenton et al., 1993). Yet despite the implied public assumptions that charitable giving is the means by which needs are met by transferring resources from the better off to disadvantaged groups, only a small percentage of charitable benefit is in fact directed to the poor and needy. In Chapter 2, we showed that the share of resources across different registered charities serving a range of different social needs varies

DOI: 10.1057/9781137522658.0008

considerably, while the distribution of specifically charitable income is particularly skewed, with large sums being concentrated in areas of activity which principally benefit, and confer social advantages on, wealthier classes (Clotfelter 1992; Odendahl 1989, 1990; Wagner, 2000).

This is not a modern phenomenon. It is historically typical that personal preferences, family connections and connections to local causes affect philanthropic decisions, and historical studies demonstrate that members of the wealthier classes have always been on the receiving end of some charitable benefit (Prochaska, 1990; Rosenthal, 1972). It is also important to note that the legal definition of charity in England and Wales refers to an organization established for exclusively charitable purposes, where the purposes must meet the requirement of public benefit (Charities Act, 2011, ss. 1–5). Some charities offer universal public benefit but the public benefit requirement can be met in relation to a clearly identified section of the public, so charities can be established to meet the needs of specific beneficiary groups. Every charity is thus constitutionally bound to address the needs of its beneficiaries – but it is up to the trustees to decide how those needs are to be addressed: there is no specific requirement for a charity to be redistributive (Morgan, 2012).

Secondly, philanthropic giving is not a one-step process involving a binary decision of 'to give' or 'not to give'. Instead it involves at least four steps. These can be summarized as follows:

1 whether or not to make a donation;
2 which cause/charitable organization will receive the donation;
3 how much to give away; and
4 what method will be used to make the gift.

Political initiatives can influence one or other of these steps – for example, an enhanced tax relief could motivate a donor to make a bigger donation than they might otherwise have considered, or a matched funding scheme for endowment building could re-direct a gift away from project funding – but donor autonomy over the other steps, notably the recipient cause, means that the final philanthropic outcome lies beyond political control. A new tax break, matched funding scheme or any other political initiative could simply lead to more funds for cause areas that are not governmental priorities. Thus, there is no guarantee that increased charitable giving would result in a better match between need and resources.

DOI: 10.1057/9781137522658.0008

Thirdly, donors value their autonomy and the freedom of giving, which they contrast favourably with the compulsory nature of taxation, sometimes on the grounds that individuals and communities are best placed to identify and meet need. This autonomy often extends to a desire to do something different to what would be funded by the money paid through the tax system. There are many types of charitably funded activity that do not have a needs-based objective nor are aligned with the priorities determined by government. The breadth of charitable giving can encompass activities that:

1 *Challenge government.* Many charities campaign against government policies or aim to prompt new governmental action. As noted in Chapter 1, some charities pioneer new activities designed to meet social needs, particularly before there is widespread agreement that such needs are legitimate; a good recent example would be the work of charities in the fields of substance abuse (Berridge and Mold, 2010). In recent years UK charities have run successful campaigns on a range of issues including cancelling the debt of poor countries, extending marriage to same-sex couples, and retaining the right to send books to people in prison. That they are successful in doing so is evident in recent efforts by government to restrict the extent of allegedly 'political' activity by charities.

2 *Cater to lifestyle interests*, albeit while pursuing a broader public good. Many charities exist to enable people to pursue their hobbies, whether those be bell ringing, beekeeping, boating, brass bands or any other pastime that people enjoy. Some might question whether such activities are genuinely charitable or whether they are simply membership associations, but many such groups can make broader contributions to the quality of life in communities.

3 *Serve niche interest groups.* Many charities exist to convene and serve like-minded people who may form a very small subsection of the population and who are therefore unlikely to find majority support for their cause. For example, as of July 2015 there are eight charities in the UK dedicated to helping vegetarians – including one whose activities include helping young vegetarians 'who are in conditions of need, hardship or distress'.[1]

Given the range of potential causes, and the breadth of activities that charitable organizations pursue, the idea that there is going to be a neat correspondence between the allocation of funds and the pattern of

DOI: 10.1057/9781137522658.0008

social needs seems implausible. As this chapter shows, individuals who donate – that is, the great majority of the adult population – do so in ways that reflect their own characteristics (social background, education and occupation, work and leisure connections, place of residence). Also crucial are philanthropic intermediaries: in other words, whether or not people are asked to give, and what sort of advice and influences they are exposed to in the processes of deciding where their philanthropic funds should be spent. The role and influence of intermediaries is discussed in Chapter 5 of this book.

The processes explored in this and the subsequent chapter are therefore likely to generate a heterogeneous charity population – and certainly not one that is well-aligned with needs. They could result in a glut of charities focused on animal welfare, amateur dramatics or heritage preservation in areas that have need of – or would prefer – more deliverers of human services and welfare; it could also certainly result in overlap and duplication. Furthermore, having a more even distribution of the quantum of donors would not correct for the distribution of *how much* those donors give, or lead to any homogeneity in *how* people give.

This chapter therefore explores philanthropic decision-making and how donors decide what to fund from the multiplicity of available options. It draws on a body of qualitative research gathered in five different studies that cumulatively include over 200 donors from a range of wealth backgrounds, including those earning too little to pay income tax as well as multi-millionaires. After a brief review of the complexity of giving decisions, the five datasets are described, along with a summary of the different methodologies involved.

The qualitative methods used here – primarily interviews – are not only important in terms of revealing the thought processes behind donations, but they are also the only feasible methods in terms of reaching certain key groups of donors. Million-pound donors by definition are scarce, are often wary of publicity, and unlikely to be included in conventional social surveys. Even the committed donors described in the study on 'how donors choose charities' are non-typical – only 5 per cent of the population said, in response to the Citizenship Survey,[2] that they had given more than £40 to charity in the preceding four weeks, with only around a quarter of 1 per cent claiming that they gave at least £100 per week. Yet these donors account for disproportionate shares of the total amounts of individual giving – nearly 9 per cent of the total in the case of the quarter per cent of people donating at least £100 per

DOI: 10.1057/9781137522658.0008

week. Thus it is important that we have an understanding of the ways in which they choose causes and allocate funding. Likewise the significance of workplace-based fundraising (and indeed, the hopes that this can be expanded, as expressed in the UK government's document *Every Business Commits* (2010)), mean that insights are needed into the processes whereby decisions are made to support (or not) particular causes.

The findings section begins with five composite case studies created by drawing on key characteristics found in each sample population, to convey the typical approaches to philanthropic decision-making amongst the different donor groups studied. This is followed by a discussion of the key themes that emerge across the whole donor population.

We reflect on the logics at play in the process of allocating funds to charities. We show that individuals engage in greater or lesser degrees of reflection, and that social needs are by no means uppermost in this process. As charitable status is available to such a wide variety of causes, this means that the outcomes are heterogeneous in the extreme. What to an individual appears a perfectly justifiable decision can result in what, in the aggregate, appears an arbitrary allocation of resources. The chapter concludes with a discussion on how this data helps with understanding the 'logic of charity' – in particular, the question of whether, and to what degree, creating a better match between philanthropic supply and demand is amenable to political influence.

The complexity of giving decisions

The majority of charities find it necessary to seek support from donors. Of the 129,000 charities in England covered in the 2008 National Survey of Third Sector organizations (Ipsos MORI, 2008), just under 100,000 declared that they received some income from donations and fundraising activities, and some 47,000 stated that these were the income source of greatest importance to the achievement of their objectives. An estimated 30,000 charities made no reference to the receipt of such funding.

There are around 200,000[3] registered charities in the UK. Not all of these will be fundraising charities: some will be grant-making and a few will be funded by an endowment, trading or other source that does not require seeking ongoing voluntary support. But the figures here suggest that some three-quarters of charities appear to be actively seeking donors, which creates a vast range of giving opportunities that is confusing for even the most diligent of donors. In this situation, North American research finds that: 'Charitable donations find their way to grantees through a haphazard combination of luck, charisma and razzmatazz that is poorly suited to the importance of their work' (Goldberg, 2009, p. 29).

As noted in the introductory chapter, there are many differences between how politicians and private donors make decisions. Political programmes and the funding decisions that arise in their implementation are the result of processes involving research, policy development and refinement, combined with processes of negotiation, compromise and collective decision-making. The allocation of funding to individual organizations (e.g., local government units, or individual hospitals) is then likely to follow relatively straightforward, needs-based criteria (although in recent years public service reforms have increasingly emphasized competitive mechanisms). And the processes underpinning such decisions are, broadly, transparent, if bureaucratic.

Philanthropic decisions are simpler: so long as the chosen recipient fits the legal definition of providing 'public benefit', the donor is free to transfer as much or as little of their private wealth as they wish. Indeed, even in the absence of a public benefit rationale, so long as it is legal, donors can still fund; they must simply forego the tax breaks available for 'approved' causes. So how do individuals – whether ordinary donors or elite philanthropists – make decisions about what to fund?

Sources of data

Between 2008 and 2014, data on over 200 charity donors was gathered in five different projects, primarily through in-depth semi-structured interviews but also through surveys and participant observations. Table 4.1 summarizes the sources of data discussed in this chapter.

In contrast to the extensive quantitative material presented in Chapters 2 and 3, this chapter is based on qualitative research which enables us to gain access to donors' interpretative understanding of their giving decisions and philanthropic actions. The research interviews were approached as 'a conversation with a purpose' (Robson, 1993, p. 228), and in all cases a semi-structured format was used, which combined specified questions with the freedom to 'probe beyond the answers ... [to] seek both clarification and elaboration on the answers given' (May, 1997,

TABLE 4.1   *Summary of five sources of data on charitable donors*

Research project and abbreviation	Date of study	Donor profile	Size of sample (N = 213)	Methodology
Annual Million Pound Donor Report[4] (MPDR)	Began 2008, ongoing	People who have made at least one single donation worth £1m+. Age range 30s–70s, most aged 50+. Majority are male and self-made	23	Case studies based on interviews
How Donors Choose Charities[5] (HDCC)	2008–10	Committed donors giving c.£10–£100/month). Age range 30s–80s, typically in 60s. Two-thirds male Equal mix of lower, middle and higher-income earners	60	Telephone interviews
Corporate Philanthropy on the Shop floor[6] (CP)	2010–11	Employees in large companies with corporate philanthropy programmes. Primarily female and low paid	10 work places (c.30 staff)	Interviews and observation
Richer Lives: why rich people give[7] (RL)	2011–13	Wealthy people: most with net worth of £10m+, making average annual donations of £300,000. Majority are aged 65+, male and self-made	82	Online survey and in-depth interviews with sub-sample of 22
Giving Circles in the UK[8] (GC)	2013–14	Members/participants in giving circles – mix of gender and wealth levels with a preponderance of young professionals	18	Interviews and observation

p. 111). In the study where case studies were created of 'million pound donors' (MPDR), these cases were written up after interviews and edited through an iterative process involving the donor.

In two of the studies – of 'shop floor' employees (CP) and of giving circle members (GC) – a small amount of data was collected through observation, which involved being present in the workplace or at giving circles, to observe discussions about how charitable causes were chosen for support.

In one study, examining 'why rich people give' (RL), a survey was used to enable collection of a larger dataset, after which a subsample was interviewed. The survey was administered using Qualtrics software and involved 40 questions, including a mix of multi-choice and open-ended questions.

The methodology for creating the five composite case studies, presented in the next section, involved analyzing each dataset to identify the key themes that emerged across the sample, and then writing them into a first person narrative that captures those points. The process of checking that these composites are sufficiently authentic, without compromising promised anonymity, and that they are accurate representations of the reality they are intended to reflect, involved sharing each composite case study with appropriate external academics who had either participated in the original data collection or have expertise in researching that donor group. This process resulted in useful amendments to all five case studies that we now present.

Findings: five composite case studies

Composite case study 1 (CCS1): million pound donor

'Lena' worked as a nurse before she and her husband made their fortune in property development.

I donated £1 million to a children's hospital because my grandson was born with a rare and complicated genetic syndrome and I wanted to do something to help. Perhaps if I had a family member with a different health problem, like autism, then I would be supporting a charity that helps autistic children instead.

That donation is staggered – I'm giving it over five years, partly for tax reasons and partly so that I can keep an eye on things. I think one has a responsibility to make sure that the funds are spent wisely. I like to meet with the researchers and doctors as I am interested in how they are getting on. They are always very open and helpful, and

DOI: 10.1057/9781137522658.0008

my training as a nurse helps me understand a little of what they are doing.

My husband and I have made a number of other large gifts, including support for scholarships at the university he attended, and for the redevelopment of our local theatre where we have enjoyed attending performances for many years. Personal reasons are the most powerful factor behind my giving. I wish I'd danced as a young woman, so we also support a project for young dancers.

In all these cases it wasn't just a case of signing a cheque but of being personally involved as a family, because we prefer to make a contribution that's about more than just money. Meeting the people we fund is more interesting than anything I do in other parts of my life.

I aim to be pioneering, not to fund 'more of the same', no matter how worthy. I like supporting those pieces of work that are either too boring or too cutting edge for the appetites of other funders. We also hope to make transformational donations – we want to know what the organization will do in a really big and meaningful way that it wouldn't have done otherwise.

Supporting good causes is something that has been a normal part of my life that started when I was a child making sandwiches on the children's ward at my local hospital. I like being busy and I couldn't just play bridge or golf every day, I need a sense of purpose. So it's not only about being altruistic because it gives me a great sense of satisfaction too.

Composite case study 2 (CCS2): committed donor of moderate wealth (HDCC)

'Richard' is in his seventies and lives in the Home Counties.

There's nothing very reasonable or logical about the things I'm compassionate about, there's no particular pattern there at all. I don't really have any definite reason for saying 'yes' or 'no' but you can't support the lot.

I've always supported charities from a young age. I've been supporting some of these charities for 40 years or more, I've got quite a good

DOI: 10.1057/9781137522658.0008

record! I support butterfly conservation because when I was a boy I collected butterflies, which meant killing them, so I'm trying to give back. That's an important one. I also support the International Glaucoma Association as I have the potential for glaucoma, detected a couple of years ago. I've had one or two leaflets that they've produced, given to me at the hospital, and I decided that they were doing a good job.

You also get other benefits from giving, sometimes just the knowledge that you have some kind of influence. It's difficult to see sometimes but if you've given £20 towards disaster relief after an earthquake, when millions are needed, it's hard to know what your influence can be, but if you know that £20 has paid for a pump or something that'd be useful in that area then that's enough to know for me. I don't really care precisely what the £20 goes to but it's good to know that it's being used.

I think definitely people both give and take, it's cyclical. I suppose I've been on the receiving end when I visit museums that have been supported by charitable donations. And I might end my days in a charitable institution, lots of people do.

I do believe that money is there to be given away. If somebody came and gave me £10,000 I would give it away because money is not much use to me. And that's more fun.

Composite case study 3 (CCS3): corporate philanthropy on the shop floor

'Anne' is the charity co-ordinator in a branch of a major supermarket.

We get a lot of colleagues saying: 'I know this charity, can we do anything for them because they helped my mum', or 'my grand-daughter has this condition'. We get that all the time, and try to help causes that are close to everyone's heart.

Cancer is always popular. You mention the word 'cancer' and it's a really big thing. Same as Children in Need, everyone wants to help children.

We don't support any charities where half the money will go for wages and admin and things like that. When the Cubs and the

DOI: 10.1057/9781137522658.0008

Scouts come in, we know that they're raising money for what they need, like going to camp or learning or whatever it is. I don't want charities coming in and raising £500 then £300 is going to pay the wages for the person who came out and did the collection. That's not something we want to be involved in.

At Easter we did some fundraising where all the managers were walking around with their faces painted. You've got to make it fun, 'cos you don't get many fun days down there, believe me. Down there on the shop floor, it's hard work. People are working constantly – they come in to do their shift, lugging boxes, putting things on the shelves, bringing things out of the chillers, and they do work hard. So it's nice to have a bit of fun, and if it raises money for charity at the same time then all the better.

I think morale would be really bad if we didn't let our hair down sometimes. If you go down the chilled meat aisle, and there's some guy standing there in a big wig and some Elton John sunglasses, raising money for a cancer charity, it's just a bit of fun, and the customers love it as well – they comment and chat to us instead of ignoring us.

Composite case study 4 (CCS4): rich donor giving a total of a seven-figure sum per annum

'John' is a self-made man in his sixties.

In order to become a serious giver, there's usually an experience like having cancer, seeing poverty or something that really triggers a meaningful commitment.

We don't have tightly drawn criteria of what sort of projects we'll fund. We will look at something new, completely afresh, and if takes our fancy then we'll do it. It's not quite as simplistic as that but it does mean we are open to new ideas.

About once a week I get an invitation to go to some event, often from some high profile person, but if I don't know that person then I just throw it away. I don't look to see what the charity is, because I'm not looking for another charity to support and this guy isn't a friend of mine. But if I get such an invitation from somebody who's

DOI: 10.1057/9781137522658.0008

in my circle, even if it's somebody I only run into every now and again, then I think: 'Well, he or she has asked me so maybe I'd better go'. And also we support one another's things, so if I go and support my friend's charity then I can phone him up and say I need him to support my charity!

If you give away large amounts of money you get increasing amounts of value from it because you can see the impact you've made. It also gets you much more access, whether it's to the actors in a theatre or to the aid workers or to the researchers in a lab, so you can get under the skin of it, which is interesting.

There is a joy in giving if you're sufficiently close to see the results, and then you get a vicarious pleasure from saying: 'I helped make that happen' – that itself is enjoyable. I have an MBE and I loved my day at the Palace. It was a very special day – I didn't do it for that but it was very nice to be recognized.

Giving is contagious, infectious, whichever word you want to use – it catches, there's nothing to beat it. There is a lot of pleasure in the relationships with those involved.

Composite case study 5 (CCS5): founding member of a giving circle (GC)

'Mary' lives in Norfolk, is upper middle class and has more disposable income since her children left home.

Giving circles appealed to me as a new way of giving. I like the openness and that it's about helping local charities and small international charities, not the big well-known charities, because everyone's already got a way of giving to them.

We hold the giving circle in a lovely venue and we give everyone a drink. Then we all sit down and each project has seven minutes to talk, and seven minutes for questions. It's very 'quick and click' and people appreciate that they're not going to have listen to somebody for half an hour! The charities leave the room and that's when we have the pledging session. People also have a form on their chair they can fill in silently, they don't have to do the open pledging.

DOI: 10.1057/9781137522658.0008

I always give more than I was intending to give. I look through the projects beforehand and say 'this one, this and this one' but I end up giving to all of them, smaller or bigger amounts, because they've presented so well, you just think: 'oh that's such a good cause – we've got to give to that!'

I don't think people are trying to out-do others in the way I imagine happens at a charity auction where you've got blokes with big personalities. I think it's the power of the presentation, the power of really feeling that you've got to know these charities, and that their representatives are so committed.

Getting up close and personal to the projects is the main driver for me, the fact that you really get to know these charities – you're told about them by the people who are delivering the service and keeping it all going, because they're very small and they don't have many resources. It's wonderful to look back over the years with some of these charities and see how they've grown and what they've done. To my mind, to be able to help charities like that – that's my motivation.

Our giving circle is popular because it's a balance between us having fun and coming together to do something good and support projects that otherwise might not get funded.

Discussion of findings: key themes

The data behind the five composite case studies provided here, consisting of in-depth, and in some cases repeated, interactions with over 200 donors, was analyzed and the following three key themes emerged:

1 *Identification*, such that donors support charitable beneficiaries with whom they identify as a result of personal connections, common experiences and shared membership of social networks.
2 *Confidence*, such that donors are motivated by having confidence in the competence of chosen charities to be efficient, effective and impactful.
3 *Enrichment*, such that donors expect – and largely receive – personal enrichment in return for their donation, unproblematically pursuing private benefits alongside public goals.

DOI: 10.1057/9781137522658.0008

Giving decisions are complex

Before describing and discussing these three themes, we begin by reiter-ating the complexity involved in giving decisions. Giving decisions are complex because of the amount of choice that is available to donors, and also because of the lack of time and ability to compare alternative recipi-ents (Breeze, 2013). We saw in the updated research on public attitudes to charity, discussed in Chapter 1, that 81 per cent of people believe that 'there are so many charities that it is difficult to decide which to give to'. This is a slight increase on the 77 per cent who agreed with that statement in 1991, and is unsurprising given that the number of registered charities in England and Wales has increased by some 25 per cent over the same period, while the mix of charitable organizations has also changed as a result of the emergence of new causes and the dissolution of many chari-ties (Backus and Mohan, forthcoming).

The qualitative data presented in this chapter both confirms and elabo-rates on that finding, as data from interviews with donors of all wealth levels demonstrates that people find giving decisions difficult. Thus despite being a committed donor, with direct debits set up to various charities, Richard (CCS2) points out that in his list of chosen charities, 'There's nothing very logical or reasonable, there's no particular pattern there at all'. Likewise, John, a donor giving more than £1 million each year, acknowledges, 'We don't have tightly drawn criteria of what sort of projects we'll fund ... if it takes our fancy then we'll do it' (CCS4).

Other donors whose phrases were not incorporated into the composite case studies said: 'it's been a bit haphazard'; '[I support] whatever catches my eye'; 'I just go by gut instinct'. Another notes, with some frustration: 'these are all worthy causes and it's very difficult, I think, to distinguish between them'. Of course there is some relation between the amounts given and the care taken to choose recipients – those giving significant sums are naturally likely to invest more time and effort into the proc-ess. There is also growing interest in concepts such as 'effective altruism', 'strategic philanthropy' and 'outcome-oriented philanthropy', whereby donors pursue evidence-based strategies to achieve the best outcome at the lowest cost per unit (Brest, 2012; Singer, 2015). Yet no donors claim it is easy to make the 'best' charitable choices, as discussed further.

Every donor in these studies supports more than one charity, but even the most prolific can only fund a tiny fraction of the tens of thousands of registered charities. So donors are not only restricted by the amount of

DOI: 10.1057/9781137522658.0008

money they have available to give away, but also by the amount of information they can gather, their ability to consider the merits of alternative recipients, and the amount of time they are able, and willing, to devote to this decision-making process. A donor who wished to consider every philanthropic option on the Register of Charities at least once a year would need to review over 350 charities every day. A donor who wished to consider every charity in their local authority area would be faced with evaluating at least three or four a week in most parts of England and Wales. The objective consideration of every conceivable option is simply beyond the capacities of individuals.

Key theme 1: identification

Despite widespread assumptions that beneficiary need is the key criterion behind giving decisions (Fenton et al., 1993), our data supports extant studies conducted outside the UK that find 'identification' between donor and recipients is crucial (Schervish and Havens, 1997; Silber, 1998, pp. 141–42). This identification is evident in the degree to which personal taste, personal preferences and autobiographical connections to causes and askers, are the most salient factors.

Personal taste and preferences are acquired as a result of lifelong processes of socialization, which include experiences of growing up within certain families and traditions, attending certain educational institutions and working in certain professional settings. As a result of these experiences, people develop affinities with particular causes and beneficiaries, which leads them to report – as the donors in our wider datasets do – that they support 'things that happen to appeal to me', causes that are 'close to my heart', things that 'touch a chord' and charities 'that I admire' and 'am comfortable giving to'. Autobiographical connections include experiences such as being affected by ill health and becoming emotionally connected to specific localities, whether this is the place they grew up, had a memorable (good or bad) experience, or currently live. Indeed one donor compared his affinity to charities in his community with loyalty to his football team.

The impact of identification is evident across the data. Lena is clear that 'personal reasons are the most powerful factor behind my giving' and that her £1 million donation to a particular health cause is attributable to her family's direct experience of it (CCS1). Similarly, the 'shop floor' donor says that causes are chosen because they are 'close to everyone's heart' as a result of touching the lives of colleagues, their families

DOI: 10.1057/9781137522658.0008

and friends (CCS3), whilst Richard supports butterfly conservation and a glaucoma charity in order to make amends for killing butterflies as a child and because he has a propensity to that eye disorder. John believes that serious givers have 'an experience like having cancer, seeing poverty, or something that really triggers a meaningful commitment'.

More data from the wider dataset that supports the salience of personal connections includes donors who support snow sports, birdwatching and steam train conservation because these are their hobbies, so 'it's my, kind of, my treat to myself, if you like' as one explains. In a similar vein, a donor from the wider HDCC dataset revels in his autonomy to indulge a taste for one animal over another: 'I would support deserving dogs but I wouldn't support cats [laughs] because I just happen not to like cats'. What have been termed 'philanthropic autobiographies' (Payton and Moody, 2008, p. 21) also have a more sombre implication for the distribution of charitable resources:

> 'My dad died unexpectedly, and mountain rescue was involved in him being brought down from the mountain, so I've given quite often to mountain rescue ... There's a personal connection'.

Likewise:

> 'My wife is blind, she [has] a guide dog ... and she gets a range of support from the Royal Institute for the Blind. I wouldn't say we wouldn't have supported blind charities if she wasn't, but obviously that gives us a particular interest in that'.

Social norms in both personal and professional settings, as well as social networks to which donors belong – or aspire to belong – can positively influence giving decisions as a result of donors identifying with fellow donors, because charitable giving is fundamentally a social act. Many donors refer to the 'normality' of giving during their upbringing and an expectation of helping behaviours in their family life. Lena (CCS1) and Richard (CCS2) had grown up as active supporters of charities in households that emphasized the importance of charitable giving.

Others referred to social norms in their peer groups that enforce a culture of giving. The public character of Mary's giving circle meant that she 'end[s] up giving to all of the [charities presenting to the circle]' (CCS5). And John expressed the understanding that norms of reciprocity are established, which can be drawn upon by others in his peer group when seeking support for their own preferred causes (CCS4).

DOI: 10.1057/9781137522658.0008

The data clearly shows that people do not give to the most urgent needs, but rather to things that mean something to them.

Key theme 2: confidence in the competence of recipient charities

The data reveals a second, non-needs-based criterion employed in giving decisions: donors' judgments regarding the competence of recipient charities to spend their contribution wisely as well as their ability and willingness to furnish evidence of its impact. Donors in our wider dataset report choosing charities on the basis of criteria such as being 'well-run' and 'efficient', or 'charities that don't pay their staff too much' and 'charities that have low overheads'.

Respondents in all five studies made numerous, unprompted comments about their fears of inefficient spending. Anne and her colleagues do not support charities 'where half the money will go for wages and admin' (CCS3), although the basis for their fears about such costs are not explained. Likewise the donor who gave £1 million wants to 'keep an eye on things' and feels 'a responsibility to make sure that the funds are spent wisely', so she expects to have access to the researchers and doctors (CCS1). Further, supporting a cause where the donor has some expertise – as with Lena, a former nurse supporting medical research – relates to the themes of both identification and confidence.

The importance of donors' perception of the performance of charities has previously been noted as a key factor in how individuals decide between competing solicitations:

> 'Donors will generally give to organizations that are both effective (in the sense that they do what they say they will do) and efficient (in the sense that they make the best possible use of the monies available to them)'. (Sargeant and Jay, 2014, p. 81)

Concerns about both effectiveness and efficiency are clearly apparent in our data, yet most donors do not use particularly sophisticated criteria against which to assess performance. One respondent noted: 'It's very difficult to sort out who uses their money well... so much of this is hearsay isn't it? Unless you pore over the books and understand what you're reading, I think it's very difficult'. Indeed, wider debate on charitable efficiency is often conducted in a fairly simplistic manner, as in the regular media furores about the salaries of senior staff in charitable organizations. No one, surely, would suggest that large organizations dealing with complex social issues, often across more than one

DOI: 10.1057/9781137522658.0008

non-European continent, should be run entirely by volunteers, or that there should be an arbitrary ceiling on the pay of such staff – yet public debate often incorporates such unreflective statements (see Mohan and McKay, forthcoming, for a discussion of the extent of 'high' salaries in the charitable sector).

An important aspect of having confidence in a charity is a belief that the donation will make a meaningful and identifiable impact that is not 'drowned out' by support from other donors or the government. Mary, the giving circle member, prefers to fund small and under-resourced causes and enjoys watching 'how they've grown' as a result of her circle's support (CCS5). Likewise, Richard is keen to know roughly what his £20 donation has paid for, in order to feel it was worth contributing in the face of great need (CCS2). In the wider dataset we see donors' concern for impact affecting their decisions in relation to the size of organization they choose to support. Some feel their money will make a splash in a smaller organization, resulting in one donor supporting a local theatre because 'it would get drowned out' if given to a national organization; whereas others take the opposite view, noting: 'I probably have gone for major charities because I feel they have more clout'.

The suggestion that donors are motivated by a desire to 'personally make a difference' has been noted as a key driver in prior studies (e.g., Duncan, 2004). We find that donors want to make meaningful contributions that are used well. This finding clearly has implications in a period when public spending on charitable activity is being cut in order to deal with the budget deficit. The expectation that voluntary income will rise to 'plug the gap' needs revising in light of the finding that donors have an expectation of 'additionality' behind their contribution. Most donors hope to make a meaningful impact beyond what would have been achieved through tax-funded measures, and there is no evidence that they are motivated to give to 'plug gaps' that arise when the state withdraws.

Key theme 3: Enrichment

The final key theme to emerge in the data is evident in all five case studies: the belief that giving is enjoyable and enriching, bringing both societal and personal benefits.

As Anne insists: 'You've got to make it fun', pointing to the role charitable fundraising plays in the workplace: 'I think morale would be really bad if we didn't let our hair down' (CCS3). John speaks of 'a joy in giving' and 'a vicarious pleasure' that comes from helping (CCS4), Lena

DOI: 10.1057/9781137522658.0008

acknowledges that her philanthropic activity brings 'a great sense of satisfaction' (CCS1), Richard insists it is 'more fun' to give money away than to keep it (CCS2), and Mary believes her giving circle strikes the right balance between 'having fun and coming together to do something good' (CCS5).

Whilst these findings support extant studies that emphasize the various personally enriching benefits of giving, including 'warm glow theory' (Andreoni, 1990), richer lives (Breeze and Lloyd, 2013) and well-being (Smith and Davidson, 2014), this is less well understood outside philanthropic circles, where debates continue as to whether the existence of personal gain – even intangible benefits such as feelings of satisfaction – detract from 'pure altruism' and make 'true gifts' impossible (Andreoni, 1990, Burlingame, 1993; Derrida, 1992).

Having highlighted the key themes in the dataset, we turn now to conclusions and implications for policymaking on philanthropy.

Conclusions

The range of studies of donation processes discussed in this chapter serve to illustrate the logic behind the supply of philanthropy. A key finding is that beneficiary demand is far less influential than donors' tastes and preferences. As Tierney and Fleishman (2011, p. 3) succinctly note: 'All philanthropy is personal'. Thus the institutional logic of philanthropy can be characterized as supply-led and influenced by factors such as identification with the cause, confidence in the charitable organization being funded, and desire for personal benefits and enrichment alongside doing good. This is not a new situation (Cunningham, 2015), and contrasts sharply with the rule-governed allocation of resources by state agencies according to democratically-agreed priorities. For this reason we should assume that the distribution of philanthropic resources will not easily change in response to new political priorities, and that it will not necessarily match the pattern of social need.

The UK has a long and proud history of charitable activity, and it has been a global economic leader for some centuries. But long-standing cultural norms relating to both giving and wealth-holding, which are viewed as private, individually driven, and only the business of the donor and potentially their family and chosen peer group – irrespective of how the donor came by their wealth – mean that philanthropy does not easily lend itself to being influenced by public policy, which operates by being public, collectively driven, and everyone's business. As Horn and Gardner (2006, pp. 83–84) note:

> [P]hilanthropy is built on the fundamental assumption that donors have a right to give away money as they see fit, just as they have a right to accumulate as much wealth as they can. Philanthropic freedom is widely celebrated... Wealthy individuals are free to support public institutions of personal importance.

The supply-driven nature of philanthropy, and the importance that donors attach to autonomy, mean that most philanthropic donations, whatever the socioeconomic position and wealth of the donors, are vehicles through which donors pursue their passions, preferences and personal enrichment, by giving to charitable organizations that have earned their confidence.

We therefore conclude that, for the most part, private giving occurs without reference to any governmental agenda and cannot be easily 'turned up' or redirected by policy levers. There are five key reasons for this:

1 *The choice of cause is largely outside the influence of political actors.* Most giving decisions are driven by personal passions and private preferences, resulting from lifelong experiences and processes of socialization, rather than as a result of a contemporary survey of the most pressing needs – which may or may not be highlighted by political actors. The way tax reliefs have been set up also militates against political influence over philanthropic choices, as the fiscal system behind charity tax breaks is almost entirely cause-neutral. This gives rise to concern that donkey charities get the same tax break as domestic violence charities (Brookes, 2010), but there has been no serious attempt to establish a 'beauty parade' of charities by politicians of any party. Therefore they have few policy levers to back up their appeals to the giving public to give more to any particular cause area, such as welfare or the arts.

2 *Political time-scales are largely incompatible with philanthropic time-scales.* Increasingly donors – especially major donors – are trying to be more strategic about their philanthropic behaviour and are making long-term, if not life-long, commitments to certain cause areas and/or charitable organizations. This can extend to donors choosing to establish an operational charity themselves, and then

DOI: 10.1057/9781137522658.0008

directing the bulk of their donations to the organization they have created. As philanthropy becomes more proactive and less reactive, there is less opportunity for appeals from anyone – including politicians – to result in an immediate response.

3   *Whilst the dividing lines are blurred, the philanthropic sector is largely defined by NOT being the private sector or the public sector.* Donor autonomy is a crucial part of the appeal of philanthropy: the ability to act freely, voluntarily and autonomously without reference to the market or the state. When the state is factored into a giving decision, it is not necessarily in a positive or complementary manner because philanthropy is sometimes motivated by anger at what the state is (or is not) doing (Silber, 2012). In this regard, the gift may be intended as a challenge to governmental policy or action, rather than a desire to support it.

Most donors do not find the time to undertake extensive research, nor are they capable of comparing the merits of every alternative recipient. Instead, people 'filter in' and 'filter out' the options, often without even realizing they are doing so. Factors that increase the likelihood of a request being 'filtered in' are the donor identifying with the cause and its beneficiaries, having confidence that their donation will make a tangible difference, and having an expectation that the process will generate some type of personal benefit.

The critique that individual donors cannot possibly evaluate all feasible options resonates with the trenchant views of Friedrich von Hayek (1944) on the ability of the state to plan and manage the economy. Hayek contended that individual choices, responding to their own preferences and to market signals, would result in an optimal outcome from the perspective of society as a whole. Pro-voluntarists make a similar argument – that it is better for resources to be allocated through individual decisions than through central planning. The freedom to distribute as much as one wants, to whom one chooses, is what distinguishes giving from paying tax.

Furthermore, the freedom to give is an essential element of a liberal society (Titmuss, 1970) and donor autonomy is a crucial factor in realizing the impulse to give (Frumkin, 2006, p. 370). Indeed, donor autonomy is paramount: people value the control they possess over their charitable giving decisions and expect to distribute their money according to their own judgments rather than in response to external signals and prompts, whether from fundraisers or politicians.

DOI: 10.1057/9781137522658.0008

The importance of donor autonomy has implications for the extent to which giving and philanthropy can be relied upon to 'fill the gaps' in meeting need. Successive governments have viewed voluntary giving as a potential resource to meet needs that the state either cannot afford, or is unwilling, to fund. In some cases this may be a successful strategy: where donors have a taste for meeting a particular need, it may well be possible to increase the flow of resources from this quarter. But given the predominance of taste-based over needs-based giving, there can be no guarantee that needs left unmet by the state will automatically be met by private individuals. Indeed, it has been noted that donors 'run away from needs' because what they are attracted by is the opportunity to 'do something special' and give to projects they are interested in (Panas, 1984, p. 116).

Creating awareness of these 'special' opportunities to arouse donors' interests is largely the job of fundraising – a profession that has grown and professionalized in recent decades as part of a growing body of intermediaries that exist between those with funds to give and those seeking resources. The next chapter will explore further the role of intermediaries such as fundraisers, and those who prompt giving decisions.

Notes

1 The Vegetarian Society, registered charity number 294767.

2 Author's analysis of Citizenship Survey, 2007–11; for details of survey, see http://discover.ukdataservice.ac.uk/catalogue/?sn=7111

3 This includes 164,916 'main charities' on the Register of Charities maintained by the Charity Commission for England and Wales, plus a further 23,942 charities registered with the Scottish Charity Regulator and between 7,000 and 12,000 estimated in Northern Ireland according to the Charity Commission for Northern Ireland (all figures from websites viewed on 26 September 2015).

4 This study is generously supported by Coutts bank. All editions of the annual reports are available online at http://philanthropy.coutts.com & http://www.kent.ac.uk/sspssr/philanthropy/whatwedo/charityresearch/couttsmilliondonor.html

5 The sample for this study was recruited with the kind help of CAF (Charities Aid Foundation). The report is available online at http://www.kent.ac.uk/sspssr/philanthropy/documents/How%20Donors%20Choose%20Charities%2018%20June%202010.pdf

6 The report is available online at http://www.kent.ac.uk/sspssr/philanthropy/documents/CP-from-the-shop-floor-Beth-Breeze-May-2013.pdf

DOI: 10.1057/9781137522658.0008

7   This study was generously supported by Pears Foundation, and co-authored by Theresa Lloyd. The key findings are freely available at https://www.dsc.org.uk/wp-content/uploads/2015/08/Look-Inside-Richer-Lives.pdf

8   This study was led by Angela Eikenberry. The full findings are available at http://www.kent.ac.uk/sspssr/philanthropy/publications/documents/growing_philanthropy.pdf

DOI: 10.1057/9781137522658.0008

5

How Intermediaries Affect the Distribution of Charitable Benefit

Abstract: *This chapter explores the role of charitable intermediaries, such as fundraisers and philanthropy advisers, in determining which causes attract – or fail to attract – philanthropic support. It begins by describing the emergence of intermediaries as a key feature of the changing philanthropy landscape over recent decades. A body of qualitative data then demonstrates that the distribution of charitable resources is skewed in favour of organizations that succeed in building meaningful relationships with donors, that give donors control over how their contributions are used and that create dual benefits by ensuring both public goods and private benefits are achieved as a result of donations. The fundamental differences between donating and paying tax are exacerbated by the intervention of charitable intermediaries, whose numbers are growing and professionalizing.*

Mohan, John and Beth Breeze. *The Logic of Charity: Great Expectations in Hard Times*. Basingstoke: Palgrave Macmillan, 2016. DOI: 10.1057/9781137522658.0009.

This chapter explores the role of charitable intermediaries in determining which causes attract – or fail to attract – philanthropic support for their beneficiaries. It builds on the finding discussed in the preceding chapter that giving decisions are affected by perceptions of charitable organizations, which in turn mediate the relationships between donors and beneficiaries.

Whilst the 'coldness' of charity has been noted by poets and politicians,[1] a positive donating experience can create the opposite temperature. 'Warm glow theory', developed by the economist James Andreoni (1990, 1993) proposes that donors get utility from the act of giving as a result of feeling good about themselves and how their act will be perceived. An illustrative example suggests:

> 'People aren't giving money merely to save the whales; they're also giving money to feel the glow that comes with being the kind of person who's helping to save the whales'. (Leonhardt, 2008)

The methods used by charitable intermediaries to 'turn up the heat' is a focus of this chapter.

Giving is usually presented as a private act, but it is almost always facilitated to some degree by others (Breeze and Lloyd, 2013, p. 174; Silber, 2012, p. 323; Sokolowski, 1996), including family, friends and peers, as well as by professionals such as fundraisers and advisers. The role and influence of intermediaries is not always apparent or recognized by donors, in part because they are (to use a gendered term) 'middlemen' who are often overlooked (Krakovsky, 2015), but also because it is viewed as more socially admirable for gifts to appear 'freely given' rather than being prompted or part of a reciprocal exchange (Derrida, 1992; Komter, 2005; Osteen, 2002). It has been suggested that in order to achieve such admiration and maintain the impression of 'free gifts', we engage in individual and collective deceptions that involve 'misrecognizing' reality, such that 'the giver and the receiver collaborate, without knowing it, in a work of dissimulation tending to deny the truth of the exchange' (Bourdieu, 1998, pp. 94–95). For example, a donor supporting a local theatre may prefer to believe themselves motivated by a belief in excellence in, and wider access to, the arts; but in reality – at least in part – they may have responded to fundraising promotions that offer special events and priority booking for donors. This misrecognition is mutually beneficial and largely harmless if it reinforces the donors' preferred sense of self and sustains a worthwhile organization. But the 'invisibility' of the

DOI: 10.1057/9781137522658.0009

context and structures within which giving occurs leads to a widespread belief that donations are largely unprompted, and makes the influence of intermediaries difficult to identify and quantify.

Types of charitable intermediaries

The most numerous type of intermediaries are fundraisers, working within an expanding and professionalizing industry (Sargeant and Jay, 2014). The UK's Institute of Fundraising has over 5,500[2] individual members, which will likely include those in more senior and settled roles, and it is estimated there are approximately 31,000 people in total currently working as fundraisers in the UK (Breeze et al 2015, p.293). The title 'fundraiser' implies a rather one-dimensional role – that of raising funds – but the job involves a much wider variety of tasks including making the public aware of the existence and legitimacy of the needs for which funds are sought, explaining how a given charity can provide a worthwhile solution and facilitating the response, which includes asking, processing donations, thanking and feeding back to donors (Breeze and Scaife, 2015, p. 572).

Understanding fundraising in this wider sense, it is less surprising that two different studies conclude that over 80 per cent of gifts are solicited (Bekkers, 2005; Bryant et al., 2003). Solicitation is also undertaken by family, friends and volunteers, but unpaid fundraisers are often unaware of the extent of professional support for their efforts. For example, a charity marathon runner using an online donation platform may think their fundraising effort is entirely voluntary, without recognizing that paid staff support volunteer fundraisers in a myriad of ways, including securing places on prestigious challenge events (such as the London marathon), providing branded goods such as t-shirts, creating online content that links to the volunteers' donation page and even turning up on the day to cheer, support and thank 'their' runners. There are also unquantifiable costs involved in building a charity's brand awareness and donor confidence to the point that it triggers volunteer's decision to raise funds for that particular cause.

In addition to fundraisers, other influential intermediaries discussed in this chapter include the senior leadership of charitable organiza- tions – their chief executives, senior managers and chairs of trustee boards – who are often the public face of their charity in media coverage and in their own communications, such as newsletters and emails. Only a minority of charities has any paid staff, but all have a chair of trustees, so in theory these intermediaries count in the hundreds of thousands (reflecting the number of registered charities). In practice, however, a much smaller number will likely be pro-actively engaged in mediating donations. We include in our discussion the nascent profession of philanthropy advisers (Leslie et al., 2015) who play a growing – though as yet unquantified – role in encouraging and distributing philanthropic expenditure (Breeze and Lloyd, 2013). These advisers provide personalized advice to major donors, either as independent consultants, or as staff members for the biggest charitable trusts and foundations, including community foundations.

We also discuss a type of intermediary based in private sector companies, who have job titles such as 'corporate philanthropy manager' and help direct private sector donations, which in 2015–16 is estimated to amount to over £650 million (Lillya et al., 2015). Finally, on a smaller, though growing, scale, we include those who host and support giving circles, as they can influence the destination of collective donations: over 80 giving circles have so far been identified in the UK, of which three-quarters are connected to a centrally organized charitable organization with dedicated professional staff (Eikenberry and Breeze, 2015). The total sums flowing through giving circles have not been quantified, but a study of the impact of membership finds it substantially increases the amounts given and strengthens long-term commitment to giving (Eikenberry et al., 2015, p. 3).

This chapter explores the role and impact of these various intermediaries in giving decisions, and argues that we cannot understand the distribution of charitable benefit without taking account of their existence and influence. The nature of the decision-making process contributes to the pattern of allocation between causes described in Chapters 2 and 3. It draws on a body of qualitative research gathered in five separate studies that cumulatively include data from over 200 intermediaries, as summarized in Table 5.3.

Most of these intermediaries focus their efforts on donors capable of making a 'major donation', which is not defined as a particular sum of money but rather as being of sufficient size in relation to the charity's needs to warrant the investment of more time and effort than would be economical for the mass of smaller donors (Lincoln and Saxton, 2012, p. 4). While the total sums raised from major donors is small in

DOI: 10.1057/9781137522658.0009

relation to total funding of the UK charitable sector of some £60 billion, the significance of major donations for individual organizations can be considerable. Such largesse can also anchor other fundraising efforts and can strengthen the charity's own competitive position through enhancing its visibility, its financial base and possibly its property base, all of which contribute indirectly to their ability to raise further funds.

After a brief review of the development and role of charitable intermediaries, the five datasets and their sources are described. The findings are organized using the same approach as in Chapter 4. Five composite case studies are presented, each drawing on the dominant characteristics found in the data relevant to that type of intermediary. A discussion of the key themes across the different populations of intermediaries then follows, and the chapter concludes with comments on how this data helps us gain a better understanding of the impact of intermediaries on the distribution of charitable benefit.

The development and role of charitable intermediaries

The defining characteristic of the modern era of charitable giving is impersonality (Zunz, 2011). The contemporary mechanisms of organized philanthropy, involving paid fundraisers and use of communication channels such as direct mail and websites, are in stark contrast to the direct, hand-to-hand transfer of resources via almsgiving that constituted charitable giving for many centuries. The introduction of intermediaries introduces an additional component, and potential skew, to the mechanisms by which private resources are redistributed to benefit the public good. As Csikszentmihalyi (2006, p. 242) notes:

> '"Philanthropoids" – as [intermediaries] are sometimes not-so-gently-called – have their own values and agendas that, consciously or not, may diverge from those of the donors and those of the recipients'.

Even when intermediaries suppress their personal agendas, there is evidence that their mere existence influences the distribution of charitable resources, with monies raised being found to relate to the degree of investment in the fundraising function, as well as to the existence of a 'culture of philanthropy' across the recipient organization, which is defined as follows:

DOI: 10.1057/9781137522658.0009

> Most people in the organization (across positions) act as ambassadors and engage in relationship-building. Everyone promotes philanthropy and can articulate a case for giving. Fundraising is viewed and valued as a mission-aligned program of the organization. Organizational systems are established to support donors. The chief executive/director is committed and personally involved in fundraising. (Bell and Cornelius, 2014, p. 17)

The existence of such a 'philanthropy friendly' culture varies across charities, with only 20 per cent of respondents in a survey of UK fundraisers agreeing that their charity has such a culture (Breeze, forthcoming).

Intermediaries can also act by omission – for example, when philanthropy advisers champion rather than challenge their clients:

> 'One of the best things that an advisor can do is say, "Your fundamental instincts are correct. It's your money, and just think of the great things you can do with it that will add to your happiness and your family's happiness."' (quoted in d'Eustachio, 2015)

In a similar vein, a handbook for philanthropists produced by Philanthropy UK recommends that advisers ask donor-centric questions such as: 'What causes do you care about?' and 'What gifts have you found most personally rewarding?' (Mackenzie, 2008, p. 14).

Of course, different philanthropy advisers take different approaches to working with clients. Many use a 'theory of change', which involves a process of logical connections between inputs, outputs and outcomes to achieve a desired – and measurable – goal, as chosen by the donor (Breeze, 2014, p. 4). Many support donors striving to become 'strategic philanthropists', which involves making the greatest impact with the available financial, and other, resources (Brest and Harvey, 2008, p. 31). However, strategic philanthropy is also cause-agnostic and accepts that 'the choice of philanthropic goals is essentially subjective' (p. 21). This approach may be consistent with contemporary principles of moral relativism, but is under increasing attack from adherents of 'effective altruism' – defined as 'a philosophy and social movement which applies evidence and reason to working out the most effective ways to improve the world' (Singer, 2015, pp. 4–5). The contemporary philosopher, Peter Singer, has done most to popularize and promote the moral case for 'cause prioritization' yet notes that effective altruists have different opinions on what counts as 'the most good' (p.7). And as so few donors are taking advantage of metrics to make utilitarian philanthropic decisions, with the vast majority of giving driven by donor commitment to a cause

DOI: 10.1057/9781137522658.0009

or locality (Schambra, 2014), seeking 'value for money' within a cause area chosen by the donor looks likely to remain the dominant approach amongst philanthropists and those who advise them (Connolly, 2011).

The emergence of philanthropy advisers is a key feature of the changing philanthropy landscape in the first decade of the twenty-first century (Breeze and Lloyd, 2013, p. 169). In their study of 82 major donors, a third (35 per cent) described the availability of better philanthropic advice as a 'significant development in UK philanthropy' in the past decade, with 'emerging' (younger and newer) donors more likely to hold this view than 'established' donors (43 per cent against 28 per cent) (p. 83). Seeking philanthropy advice was also far more common and acceptable among the newer donors, as shown in Table 5.1: while three-quarters (73 per cent) of the established group had not sought advice and only 11 per cent might do so in future, a third (33 per cent) of emerging donors had already sought such advice and a further fifth (21 per cent) see it as a viable option in the future. In total, just over a quarter (28 per cent) of all respondents had sought philanthropy advice, and in most cases that advice had influenced their giving plans.

To clarify further the role and influence of philanthropy advisers, Table 5.2 lists the main benefits sought by those paying for philanthropy advice.

TABLE 5.1   *The incidence and impact of seeking philanthropy advice*

Have sought philanthropy advice?	Impact on giving plans	% of all donors	% of 'established' donors	% of 'emerging' donors
No	Not applicable: 'I have not sought philanthropy advice on my giving from a professional adviser'	56	73	40
No	Not applicable: 'I have not sought philanthropy advice but might do so in the future'	16	11	21
Yes	Yes: 'I have sought philanthropy advice and it has influenced my giving plans'	24	14	33
Yes	No: 'I have sought philanthropy advice but it did not influence my giving plans'	4	3	5

Source: Breeze and Lloyd (2013, p. 173).
Reproduced with the kind permission of the Directory of Social Change (DSC) www.dsc.org.uk.

DOI: 10.1057/9781137522658.0009

TABLE 5.2   *Type of philanthropy advice requested*

Type of philanthropy advice requested	% of philanthropy advisers being asked for this service
Personalized discussion of their philanthropic interests, with tailored solutions on how their giving might be structured	75
Signposting to materials produced by other organizations that support donors	67
Introductions to other donors who share their interests	67
Management of clients' philanthropy, including relationships with beneficiaries, project visits, assessment of feedback reports etc.	58
Recommendations of books and articles	50
The provision of training on strategic philanthropy	42
Introductions to external philanthropy specialists	33
Suggestion as to which charities they might support within their areas of interest	25
Introductions to potential beneficiaries	25

Source: Breeze and Lloyd (2013, p. 178).
Reproduced with the kind permission of the Directory of Social Change (DSC) www.dsc.org.uk

Advisers are greatly outnumbered by fundraisers, whose wider role in framing, facilitating and reinforcing charitable transactions was noted earlier. A study of 'fundraising for unpopular causes' underlines the importance of well-resourced and skillful fundraising and communication efforts in achieving success in generating voluntary income for even the most challenging causes (Body and Breeze, 2015). People intuitively understand that some causes are easier to fundraise for than others, but this study contains examples of successful solicitation for charities working with beneficiaries that lack widespread or instinctive support – such as prisoners, addicts and asylum seekers – as a result of strategies such as being proactive in asking, investing in fundraising, empowering cheerleaders, focusing on donor retention rather than recruitment and ensuring donors understand the impact of their donation (pp. 41–42).

Implementing a successful fundraising programme is not necessarily related to the extent or urgency of the need being served; nor is there any reason why 'good asking' would be equitably distributed in terms of geography. Yet the importance of these factors may well exacerbate extant distributive patterns by favouring richer organizations that can afford to invest in fundraising, development and communication professionals,

DOI: 10.1057/9781137522658.0009

and other non-frontline roles that help to raise an organization's profile and attract donations.

The different types of charitable intermediaries are, or course, not equivalent. Charity managers and fundraisers are employed by charities to deliver their mission and secure resources; corporate philanthropy managers are employed by private companies that are ultimately responsible to shareholders; philanthropy advisers are paid by individual donors, either directly or indirectly – for example, as part of banking charges; and giving circle hosts may be funded either by their members or by a charity hoping to benefit from members' contributions. Yet differences extend beyond 'who pays the bills' and 'who hopes to benefit'.

Whilst intermediaries are so called because they seek to simultaneously meet the needs of two parties (donors and recipients), different intermediaries are more closely aligned with one or other party. The chairs and chief executives of charities are legally obliged to promote the interests of their organization and beneficiaries, whilst philanthropy advisers and corporate philanthropy managers must prioritize the interests of the funders they represent in order to make their roles sustainable. Fundraisers and giving circle hosts are most often employed by charities, though they may also operate as freelance consultants; but in either case they often characterize themselves as 'double agents', representing the needs of the charity to the donor and representing the needs of the donor to the charity (Breeze, forthcoming).

With the emergence of these roles, the impact of achieving a reputation as a competent charitable organization extends beyond positively influencing individual giving decisions. Being a recognized, trusted 'charity brand' with a successful fundraising department may also help to secure partnerships with private sector companies, inspire recommendations from philanthropy advisers, and increase the opportunities to present to giving circle members. How the influence of these various intermediaries impacts on giving decisions and skews the distribution of donations, is the focus of this chapter.

Sources of data

Between 2008 and 2014, data on over 200 charitable intermediaries was gathered in five different projects, using a range of methodologies

DOI: 10.1057/9781137522658.0009

including an online survey, interviews, case studies and observations. Table 5.3 summarizes the sources of data discussed in this chapter. Full information on the methodologies used in each study are available in the longer published versions, as indicated in the footnotes.

TABLE 5.3   *Summary of sources of data on charitable intermediaries*

Research project and abbreviation	Date of study	Sample profile	Size of sample (total = 209)	Methodology
Annual Million Pound Donor Report[a] (MPDR)	Began 2008, ongoing	Fundraisers in charities that have received at least one single donation worth £1m+	17	Case studies based on interviews
Who Gives, Who Gets[b] (WGWG)	2012	Chief executives, chairs, and senior managers in charities	149	Online survey, follow up case studies based on interview with subsample of 6
Richer Lives: why rich people give[c] (RL)	2011–13	Professional philanthropy advisers: half based in banks, the rest in legal firms or independent advisers.	12	Online survey
Giving Circles[d] in the UK (GC)	2013–14	Staff/paid hosts of giving circles, based in charities, and community foundations	21	Interviews and observation
Corporate Philanthropy on the Shop Floor[e] (CP)	2011–12	Managers in large companies with corporate philanthropy programmes	10	Interviews

Notes: [a] This study is generously supported by Coutts bank. All editions of the annual reports are available online at http://philanthropy.coutts.com & http://www.kent.ac.uk/sspssr/philanthropy/whatwedo/charityresearch/couttsmilliondonor.html
[b] The sample for this study was recruited with the kind support of ACEVO (Association of Chief Executives of Voluntary Organizations); research assistance was provided by Eddy Hogg
[c] This study was generously supported by Pears Foundation, and co-authored by Theresa Lloyd. The key findings are freely available at https://www.dsc.org.uk/wp-content/uploads/2015/08/Look-Inside-Richer-Lives.pdf
[d] This study was led by Angela Eikenberry. The full findings are published in Eikenberry and Breeze (2015)
[e] The report is available online at http://www.kent.ac.uk/sspssr/philanthropy/documents/CP-from-the-shop-floor-Beth-Breeze-May-2013.pdf

DOI: 10.1057/9781137522658.0009

Findings

Composite case study 6 (CCS6): million pound recipient

'Anya' is fundraising director of one of the UK's biggest charities.

Fundraising is all about building meaningful relationships, and that can take years to develop before a transformational gift occurs. Listening is crucial – it's very easy for fundraisers to keep trying to 'sell' their organization and forget to listen to donors and really understand what interests them. It's also important to understand that they can – and want – to give more than just money: they have ideas, expertise, time and contacts to share. We don't see them just as funders, we start by saying: 'what can we achieve together?'

People usually start with a smaller gift and give more as they get to know us and have increased engagement with our work. Major donors want to understand fully how their donations will be deployed and they want their support to be in line with their personal interests and affinities. We're very aware of this and ensure we have a bespoke approach when it comes to building relationships with each and every single one of our significant supporters.

No two major donors are the same, they all want different things and we do the best we can to ensure their philanthropic experiences are exactly how they would wish them to be. Donor care at this level includes access to our leadership, appropriate naming opportunities and regular visits to projects – there is nothing more fulfilling for a donor than to see their gift in action. Through all our interactions we try to create memories for donors and their families that last forever, so that their relationship with us will also last a lifetime.

One big donation can also open the door to others, it helps us start conversations with other potential donors if someone they respect is already supporting us. It sends out a reassuring message that we are viewed by their peers as deserving of, and capable of managing, serious money. Our most recent seven–figure donor has a philanthropy adviser who was so impressed by dealing with us and seeing the difference the money made, that he is now happy to talk about us to other clients.

DOI: 10.1057/9781137522658.0009

Major donors are incredibly important because they help us to trail-blaze, to test and trial different ways of working. The charity sector is very effective at innovation and finding ways to solve problems. Philanthropists are the people who help to fuel innovation.

Composite case study 7 (CCS7): Who Gives, Who Gets

'Jean' is CEO of a medium-sized homelessness charity that is attached to a major Christian church.

We are a faith-based charity that helps all kinds of people affected by homelessness. Many of our donors support us as a way of express-ing their religious beliefs. They want to reach out to people in need and they also understand that the people we help are not that unlike them – we are all just one redundancy or one unpaid bill away from potentially being homeless.

We make significant efforts to ensure that all our donors are given information on our work, and have access to our organization. For example, we send out a newsletter four times a year, and we invite donors to visit our building where they can meet staff and volun-teers – but not the people we help as we must protect their privacy. Our 'open door policy' helps us to attract donors because everyone who gives, be it £5 or £5,000, wants to see how their donation has made a difference.

Our most committed donors often have a longstanding historical connection with the cause or with our organization; they them-selves or, more often, their parents may have grown up in the area we serve, and are therefore inclined to donate to us.

A lot of our fundraising activity occurs through our community fundraising programme which encourages local churches, schools, Rotary groups, Scout and Guide groups and other community organizations to hold fundraising events to support us. Participants in these events often become individual donors, which helps build our loyal core support.

When we get funding for projects it tends to reflect the particular interests and concerns of the donor. For example, they might believe that education is a very important issue and a factor behind

DOI: 10.1057/9781137522658.0009

homelessness, so they send money that is only to be spent on our educational activities.

If the local media publishes an article about our work, that often results in people sending money specifically to help the person featured in that story because donors like to be able to picture who they are helping.

Composite case study 8 (CCS8): Richer Lives – philanthropy advisers

'Rachel' works in the philanthropy advisory team of a major private bank.

My typical clients are in their fifties or sixties, self-made and financially secure. Having taken advice when generating and managing their wealth, they are comfortable with the idea of professional input for distributing it.

My job is to help them work out how their wealth can most effectively make a positive difference – whether that is in a community they belong to, a cause that has affected them or an issue they feel strongly about.

In the main philanthropic decisions are personal and are affected by the traditions and values with which people were brought up and by incidents that happen during their lifetime. The focus of their giving varies from person to person. Each individual or family has their own unique reasons and motivations for giving and ways of doing things.

If a client is uncertain about where to start, we might begin by discussing some basic question such as: 'Are there any charitable interests you would like to support?' or, 'Have you supported charities in the past?'

Donors don't generally feel the need to consult experts when deciding whether or not to donate to their old school or university, or to an art form that they love, but they may want help in situations where they lack 'insider knowledge'. The top three cause areas that my clients raise are international development, human services and welfare, and education outside of universities, particularly for disadvantaged children.

DOI: 10.1057/9781137522658.0009

Clients want to see what their funding is achieving and want to keep control of how their money is spent – both these factors are drivers for lifetime giving rather than giving on death. Of those who leave charitable bequests, most name charities that they have already supported during their lifetimes, and about a third want to either establish or 'top up' a personal foundation.

I think that clients are receptive to the view that they should get the pleasure and enjoyment of making lifetime gifts, whether to existing charities or to foundations which they set up. There's also a desire to participate and get involved with the recipients, rather than just write a cheque, as well as a desire to involve their family in their philanthropy.

Composite case study 9 (CCS9): hosts of giving circles

'Jasmin' is employed to support a network of giving circles around the UK.

Joining a giving circle is a good option for the mass affluent, for those who want to do more than support their mate who's running a marathon. We think giving should be somewhere between a gesture and a sacrifice and if you can only afford £50 or £100, it's much better to pool money with others to support a charity properly.

Almost all our members already support a 'big brand' charity so giving through a circle is a way for them to find out about smaller, start-up organizations that are often more innovative.

Our members like projects where their money goes a long way, so international development, especially education projects in Africa, Asia and Eastern Europe, are always popular. People are also very interested in supporting projects in their own community. They occasionally pick tough causes like sex trafficking, but often go for things that will be an easier sell, more motherhood and apple-pie rather than grittier causes.

Some causes always do well: children and education are a no-brainer. Refugee charities will do a solid amount, as will domestic violence charities – even when they pitch to a circle that's mostly male members, because they have daughters.

The ones that bomb, it's not because of the cause but because the presenter hasn't managed to communicate their passion, or isn't the person on the ground. Our members say 'it's clear you like this cause but somehow you're failing to move me'. Founders are very powerful presenters because they have the passion, and when beneficiaries present that can go very well too.

The number one thing that donors are scared of is their money being wasted, so they don't tend to support projects when it's not clear how the money will be spent and it isn't clear what the impact might be. Charities need to explain how they will know if the project has succeeded or not

We want to make the circle a proper community where people are not just coming for charities, they're coming for each other. Some giving circles are really friendship groups first and foremost. Occasionally we organize events without any charities pitching – it's just a social occasion, perhaps to celebrate a successful year.

Composite case study 10 (CCS10): corporate philanthropy manager perspective

'Duncan' is manager of Corporate Philanthropy in a FTSE100 firm.

Helping charity is never going to be our core business. I get it from a moral point of view, but we always have to think: how does it help the company?

We are directed by a business need to be visually active in certain areas. In terms of our corporate image, the company wants to have a national charity partner that the public is aware of. And as we have branches around the country, we also want to support the communities that we are based in, where our staff and customers live. It's basically showing to the public – nationally and locally – that we care.

Corporate philanthropy used to be like a one-night stand, involving a press release and a big charity cheque. But now we prefer long-term, strategic partnerships with charities that are aligned with our business. Charity partners need to speak our language and fit in with the culture and ethos of our company and play to our strengths.

DOI: 10.1057/9781137522658.0009

They also need to keep it fresh by having different aims and focus for each year of the partnership. Let's be honest – there'll always be a commercial rationale behind our choice of charity partner and there are certain charities we would steer away from if they were going to cause us issues.

We're looking for win-win scenarios including exciting and inventive ways to develop our people. We look to the third sector for non-traditional skills development that increases our employees' morale and sense of achievement, and offers meaningful and memorable opportunities. Charity partnerships can also help us to meet potential clients in a different way.

Every relationship needs to involve fun, and fundraising is a fantastic team-building vehicle. At company fundraising events, barriers are taken down and everyone rolls their sleeves up – there's no 'I'm the area director so I'll take the lead'. We all have a good laugh and discover some hidden talents, whilst extending networks across the company and doing something for charity at the same time.

Discussion of findings: key themes

The dataset lying behind the five composite case studies provided here, which contains interactions with 209 charitable intermediaries, was analyzed, and the following three key themes were identified:

1   *Relationships*, such that intermediaries create and develop meaningful, long-term relationships that take account of the individual interests, needs and aspirations of potential donors.
2   *Donor-centred*, such that intermediaries enable donors to earmark their contributions for the aspect of the charity's work they feel most strongly about, and are shown evidence of the impact of that expenditure.
3   *Dual benefits*, such that intermediaries serve both the donor and the recipient, ensuring that both public goods and private benefits (of various types) are achieved as a result of the donation.

Key theme 1: relationships

The truism that 'people give to people' is reflected in the emphasis on building and developing meaningful relationships with donors that

DOI: 10.1057/9781137522658.0009

appears in all the composite case studies. Anya says, 'Fundraising is all about building meaningful relationships', which requires a 'bespoke approach' in order to understand each donor's 'personal interests and affinities' (CCS6). The philanthropy adviser Rachel says that her clients are seeking relationships with those they support, having 'a desire to participate and get involved with the recipients, rather than just write a cheque' (CCS8). And Duncan describes a shift in choosing corporate charity partners from 'one-night stands' to 'long-term, strategic partnerships' (CCS10). Another fundraiser, whose quotation was not incorporated into the composite case studies, underlines the crucial role of building strong relationships: 'Million pound donors don't come out of the blue. Donations of that size only come as a result of long-term relationships and from our most loyal supporters'.

'Relationship Fundraising' has been a dominant approach advocated in the fundraising profession since the early 1990s (Burnett, 2002). This approach argues that charitable donations are fundamentally different to financial transactions conducted in the spheres of business and government, because donors should be viewed as friends, not customers or taxpayers. Anya in CCS6 says, '[W]e start by saying: "what can we achieve together?"' A project leader in the wider MPD study explains, 'I have developed a good friendship' with a man who eventually gave a multi-million pound donation. As friends, donors want to be known and understood and to be included on the 'inside track', which means being properly informed, appropriately involved and given the chance to participate actively in the charity's work. This relationship-based approach is contrasted to 'transactional' approaches which involve one-off, one-way financial transactions that lack the personal investment of 'many of the highest human emotions' that typifies successful fundraising (Ibid., p. 2).

The downside of this approach is that it can be challenging for charities lacking staff and supporters with the right contacts to break into the charmed circles inhabited by the kind of donors with whom they wish to develop relationships. Furthermore, there are costs and risks involved in investing in developing personal relationships that may not culminate in achieving the size of gift anticipated – knowing when to stop 'cultivating' a potential donor is a difficult call to make, especially when that decision involves writing off the time and costs invested thus far.

DOI: 10.1057/9781137522658.0009

Key theme 2: donor-centred

Relationship fundraising shares many similarities with 'donor-centred fundraising' (Burk, 2003), which advocates focusing on the people making gifts rather than on the gifts they make, in order to develop respectful and enjoyable relationships that will last for the long-term. A more equivocal perspective is offered by Daly (2011, p. 1084) who argues:

> 'These bodies [private banks offering philanthropy advice] espouse the type of "donor driven" and "individualised orientation" to philanthropy, which Ostrander (2007: 365) argues enhances the development of donor-controlled philanthropy'.

Being donor-centred involves starting with the donors' interests, needs and aspirations, and giving them as much control as possible over the process, such as the means and frequency of communication and how their money will be spent. Philanthropy advising is obviously donor-centred, as it exists to serve the needs of donors seeking professional help with their charitable giving. The donor-centric nature of philanthropy advising is noted here, and is well encapsulated in the words of a US adviser who begins by asking donors: 'when you wake up at night, what are you worrying about?' (quoted in d'Eustachio, 2015).

The donor-centric theme is evident across our five studies. Rachel explains that her '[c]lients want to see what their funding is achieving and want to keep control of how their money is spent' (CCS8); indeed an adviser in the wider Richer Lives dataset says her clients are often 'control freaks' in both their business and their philanthropic activities. The 'Guide to Giving', a best practice handbook for donors and their advisers, states that 'there is no "right" strategy or "right" portfolio – it is a question of what matters to you' (Mackenzie, 2008, p. 13) and suggests 'effective giving' involves 'mak[ing] a difference to causes you care about' (p. 14). A website designed to support and advise donors, similarly states that:

> '[t]he first stage of giving is to think about what *you* want to achieve-giving becomes rewarding when it reflects *your* beliefs and when you can see what you are accomplishing'.[3] (emphasis added)

The mainstreaming of 'donor-centred fundraising' amongst those working with major donors is exemplified by Anya, who explains that the donors supporting her charity 'all want different things and we do the best we can to ensure their philanthropic experiences are exactly how they would wish them to be', which includes ensuring they 'fully understand how their donations will be deployed' (CCS6).

Donor control is clearly apparent in the earmarking of many donations for restricted spending, rather than contributing to the general operating budget and trusting the charity's staff and trustees to spend it as appropriate. Examples of earmarked donations appear across the data. For example, Jean explains that her homelessness charity receives donations which can only be spent on specific projects that 'reflect the particular interests and concerns of the donor', and that media coverage can resulted in donations directed specifically at the homeless person featured in that story (CCS7). Jasmin explains that giving circle members withhold donations from charities that cannot explain exactly how their contribution will be spent and what it will achieve (CCS9).

Donations can also be earmarked in a territorial sense, with both Jean and Rachel (CCS7, CCS8) referring to donors' support for communities to which they belong, which imparts a geographical bias to the distribution of donations, as noted in Chapter 3. In a country in which rich and poor are becoming increasingly segregated, the ability of charitable funding to reach communities that need it most can be questioned.

Key theme 3: dual benefits

Despite widespread assumptions that charitable giving involves one-way transactions from rich to poor, a key insight of the nascent discipline of philanthropic studies is that it is a defining characteristic, and historically typical, for philanthropy to meet the needs of both the donor and those they support (see, e.g., Fleishman, 2007; Frumkin, 2006; Payton and Moody, 2008).

The search for 'dual benefits' is a strong theme in our findings. Duncan, the corporate philanthropy manager, says that when choosing a charity partner he is 'looking for win-win scenarios' that 'help the company', such as 'fun' team-building activities and 'exciting and inventive ways to develop our people' (CCS10). The giving circle creates social benefits for members such that 'people are not just coming for charities, they're coming for each other' (CCS9), and the philanthropy adviser acknowledges that her clients seek 'pleasure' and 'enjoyment' when making gifts (CCS8).

DOI: 10.1057/9781137522658.0009

The relationship-building and donor-centred techniques used by major donor fundraisers, described in this chapter, generate private benefits, as explained by Anya: 'Through all our interactions we try to create memories for donors and their families that last forever' (CCS6). Other major donor fundraisers in our dataset describe specific donor benefits they offer, including trips to visit projects overseas, naming opportunities and interactions with royalty and celebrities. Similar efforts to generate donor benefits for non-rich donors are described by Jean whose charity sends out regular newsletters and offers an 'open door policy' for donors giving as little as £5 (CCS7).

The idea that those with resources to spare should also benefit from charitable transactions may strike some people as unnecessary at best, and as unwisely – even unethically – exacerbating existing advantage at worst (Reich, 2005, 2006; Ostrander, 2007). But seeking dual benefits, or 'win-wins', is a typical tactic of charitable intermediaries; and those able to offer the most enticing and enjoyable donor benefits will do so to the advantage of some charities and not others, thus impacting on the distribution of charitable benefit.

Conclusions

In the context of discussing corporate support for the arts, Stead (1985) described a shift from 'cold contributions' to 'warm contributions'. The former involves giving cash to 'faceless beneficiaries' whilst the latter involves giving money, personal time and other resources to known beneficiaries. This typology can be usefully applied to our study of charitable intermediaries, who 'heat up' the input of donors, transforming cold cash transfers into 'warm contributions' by engaging donors, enabling them to give more than money and ensuring they either meet beneficiaries or understand enough about the projects they are funding to be able to picture satisfactorily the impact of their support.

The 'warm glow' theory of charitable giving proposes that donors get utility from the act of giving as a result of feeling good about themselves and how their act will be perceived (Andreoni, 1990). The 'glow' from giving does not automatically occur, and the data presented here demonstrates that one role of intermediaries is to ensure that donors achieve this state.

DOI: 10.1057/9781137522658.0009

In contrast, transfers of money through tax receipts and public spending are inevitably 'cold'. Taxpayers can only contribute cash; they have minimal, if any, understanding of what their personal contribution achieves; and the process is not viewed as enjoyable or enriching, even by the most fervent advocates of high taxation. However enthusiastic a taxpayer is about an item of public expenditure and however big their tax bill, they cannot earmark their contribution for spending on that item, nor will – or should – they receive a personal invitation to 'get close' to the impact of the funded good or service.

Donating is fundamentally different to paying tax, and the essential differences – as set out in Table 1.1 in Chapter 1 – are exacerbated by the intervention of charitable intermediaries. As these intermediaries grow in number and status due to the rapid professionalization of fundraising (Bloland, 2002) and the growth of new industries such as philanthropy advising, the experience of being a taxpayer and being a donor will grow ever more distinct and different. Political hopes that voluntary income will emerge to fill public spending gaps or to fund pet programmes are unlikely to be realized until this experiential difference is understood and factored into efforts to secure private contributions.

Public spending constraints must also be factored into intermediaries' encouragement of donors' desire to 'innovate' and 'trailblaze' (CCS6), which prompts the question: If major donors enjoy funding novelty, who will continue paying for effective interventions that are – or become – old hat? It is a perennial challenge for the charitable sector to scale up pilot projects, and to find ongoing funding for projects that attracted enthusiastic private support for the capital costs. In previous decades, the state might have had sufficient resources to pick up and sustain proven initiatives; but expectations that private donors can be encouraged to enjoy the pioneering process and then hand over the reins must be tempered in a time of austerity.

Drawing together data from this chapter and the preceding chapter, we can see that donors are not interested in 'plugging gaps' in public spending. Rather they are open to invitations to become involved with causes they *identify* with, if they have *confidence* in the relevant charitable organization and find the experience of donating personally *enriching*. Their likelihood of acting on this invitation is heightened when they encounter charitable intermediaries who succeed in building meaningful *relationships*, enabling donors to *control* their contribution and achieve *dual benefits* in the public and private spheres.

DOI: 10.1057/9781137522658.0009

The corollary of these findings is that charities are going to find it harder to secure voluntary support when their cause is not one with which potential donors readily identify, when their organization does not command general confidence, when they cannot – or will not – offer the opportunity to 'earmark' donations or provide enriching donor benefits, and when they are based in geographical locations where there are fewer people with wealth and cultural capital to engage.

In the next, and final, chapter we reflect on these conclusions, as well as those reached in the preceding three chapters, to reiterate our argument on the 'logic of charity' and how it relates to political promises.

Notes

1   In a love letter to Lady Caroline Lamb, Lord Byron refers to himself as being 'as cold as charity'; in his book *The Social Worker*, written in 1920, the future prime minister Clement Attlee wrote: 'charity is a cold, grey, loveless thing'.
2   According to the Institute of Fundraising website (viewed 26 September 2015).
3   http://www.philanthropy-impact.org/setting-objectives/setting-objectives-test

DOI: 10.1057/9781137522658.0009

6
Conclusion: Where the Logic of Charity Might Lead Us

Abstract: *This book has illustrated how the logic of charity plays out, in terms of the distribution of resources across causes and communities, and the processes behind philanthropic decision-making. Whilst 'nudge' policies and place-based initiatives might eventually irrigate some so-called charity deserts, shifting the philanthropic dials will not be straightforward, either in terms of raising overall levels of giving, or creating significant shifts in the distribution of donations between causes or geographical areas. We note grounds for optimism regarding the continued vitality of charity despite adverse economic circumstances, but conclude that charities still have to work to command the confidence of the public, and to contend with the lack of political understanding of, and appreciation for, the diverse roles they play in building a pluralistic civil society.*

Mohan, John and Beth Breeze. *The Logic of Charity: Great Expectations in Hard Times*. Basingstoke: Palgrave Macmillan, 2016. DOI: 10.1057/9781137522658.0010.

We introduced this book by distinguishing the underlying organizational principles and practices of charitable activity. We subsequently illustrated how the logic of charity plays out, in terms of the distribution of resources across causes and communities (Chapters 2 and 3), and also in terms of the processes whereby individuals choose to support charities, and the ways in which those processes are managed by intermediaries (Chapters 4 and 5).

The charitable sector in England and Wales is large and very diverse, and while public attention and media coverage focus on the very large charities at the top of the income distribution, the typical charity is small, with a median expenditure of around £13,000, local, and focused on 'nice to have' activities that contribute broadly to community well-being. But when one delves below the aggregate figures we find great variation. In these circumstances, speaking of a charitable 'sector' as if it were a homogenous entity is illusory.

It is also very clear that charitable organizations are no longer, if they ever were, funded solely by private donations. Whether we can return to such an idealized scenario – as implied by William Shawcross or Nick Seddon (Chapter 2) – is debatable. Indeed whether their normative suggestions, which would reduce the scale of the 'true' charity population and its activities substantially, are at all desirable is a matter for debate. There are causes that, despite being acknowledged as significant social needs, have always struggled to obtain charitable donations. The valuable contributions made by organizations in those fields would be placed at risk if they lost the benefits of charitable status as a result of policy interventions.

The logic of charity has always entailed idiosyncrasy and particularism, and a consequence has been variations in the distribution of resources between communities. There is some truth in statements about 'charity deserts', but simplistic comments about ratios of charities to population do not do justice to a complex situation (Chapter 3). More nuanced analyses show that gaps between communities in the distribution of charities and expenditures narrow, but are not eliminated, when we make some effort to account for the geographic communities served by charities. Work on neighbourhood charities indicates the very substantial gaps that exist between the most well-resourced and most disadvantaged communities. Strong associations with material deprivation point us towards resource-based explanations of variations in the distribution of charities, rather than accounts which come close to blaming communities for not forming enough organisations.

DOI: 10.1057/9781137522658.0010

The processes explored in this book do not mean that the allocation of resources is frozen for all time. But if identification, empathy, socialization and biography, as well as connections with organizations in one's place of residence (Chapter 4), are all crucial to securing support from private donors, then shifting the philanthropic dials will not be straightforward. If connections with birthplace or current place of residence are influential, it is obviously not possible to move individuals around communities so that they are exposed to other claimants for their charitable largesse. Nor can one separate individuals from the biographical events that have influenced their choice of causes in the hope that they will favour others. Despite the arguments made by proponents of 'effective altruism', almost all giving continues to be driven by personal and local factors rather than by utilitarian calculations (Schambra, 2014). In Chapter 5 we explored the role and influence of a range of charitable intermediaries including fundraisers and philanthropy advisers. Successful fundraising is largely related to the extent of institutional investment in that function and the deployment of professional skills – particularly in building meaningful relationships with donors – rather than being a function of the extent or urgency of the need being served. The role of intermediaries, therefore, does not seem likely to contribute to a significantly more equitable distribution between causes and communities; nor is there any obvious reason why 'good asking' would be equitably distributed in terms of geography. Philanthropy advising is an emerging intermediary role that can help clients take a more 'strategic' approach to reaching philanthropic goals, but is largely silent on the selection of those goals; advisers tend to support – rather than challenge – donors' pre-existing philanthropic preferences. Aside from the generic challenge of raising overall levels of giving, discussed in the next section, our evidence indicates that significant shifts in the distribution of donations between causes or geographical areas seem likely to be difficult to achieve.

Is the glass half full or half empty?

Nevertheless, there are grounds for optimism about the continued vitality of charity. Long-run studies show that even in the heyday of the Keynesian welfare state after the Second World War, many voluntary organizations continued to be established to respond to emerging social needs and challenges (Backus and Mohan, forthcoming). Charity

DOI: 10.1057/9781137522658.0010

Commission registration statistics are an imperfect guide, influenced by changes in registration thresholds and other criteria: but – as noted in Chapter 1 – there are certainly signs of continued growth in the numbers and resources of charitable organizations.

In relation to individual giving, studies of 30 years of household expenditure survey datasets show a small reduction in the proportion of households giving to charity, but this is balanced by an increase in the average amounts given, so that the sums raised have been broadly stable or increasing slightly. Having said that there are also suggestions of generational reductions in giving when recent birth cohorts are compared against their older predecessors (Smith, 2012), potentially posing a challenge for the future. Interpreting such sources can be contentious. It is possible that these surveys underestimate funds received by charitable organizations, because the questions they ask may not reflect novel ways of giving to charity, such as by text and via online giving platforms. Information from other sources, such as NCVO's annual Almanacs, which capture information from annual reports and accounts of charities, suggests that donative income is also relatively stable.

Other evidence suggests that giving to charity recovers from adverse economic circumstances. Long-run data on individual giving from the USA, covering the interwar Depression years, suggests that the proportion of income given to charity by individuals filing tax returns remained broadly consistent, but the problem for charitable organizations was that fewer people were in work. Once the economy recovered, though, individuals resumed their donations. It is therefore reasonable to suppose that as the health of the economy improves, so too will the amounts donated (Mohan and Wilding, 2009), though whether this will be associated with changes in the pattern of charitable resource allocation remains to be seen.

An adverse economic climate (and, in the present circumstances, austerity) will impact on the finances of charities, but we cannot easily generalize about those impacts, which will depend on the balance of income sources on which organizations draw, and therefore their exposure to particular funding streams, their asset base and their policy towards investment of assets. Interwar commentators referred to the 'thousand separate Exchequers' of the voluntary hospital system: the aggregate position concealed great variation, and surpluses for organizations in some areas coincided with deficits elsewhere (Gorsky et al., 2002).

DOI: 10.1057/9781137522658.0010

In the present day, reductions in public funding will certainly affect many charities, but these influences will also be mediated by a number of factors including internal management capacity, the quality of decision-making and the extent of existing resources as well as the external environment. In the latter regard, despite the emphasis in public debate on austerity, the value of one particular tax relief – on non-domestic rates for charities – has actually gone up by some £500 million since 2010 (HMRC, 2015, figure 2.2). This is an aggregate figure and will hide variations but it does compensate at least in part for reductions elsewhere. The great majority of organizations will survive, but for some, especially those facing very real budget constraints as a result of substantial losses of public funding, these conclusions will of course seem overly optimistic.

In the tough climate of recent years, messages about stability may be reassuring, but shouldn't the dials on giving really have shifted by now? For over three decades economic policies have concentrated wealth in fewer and fewer hands, and reduced the tax burden on individuals substantially, whilst a range of policies – most notably the introduction of ever more generous charity tax reliefs, but also other efforts including social marketing, matched funding and 'nudging' – have sought to encourage and incentivize private donations. In this regard, relative stability in charitable giving might be a mark of failure. The Labour MP Frank Field began his 2015 speech to the Charity Commission by repeating an anecdotal conversation involving former Prime Minister Margaret Thatcher, which encapsulates this point:

> '"What was your greatest disappointment in government?" Back shot Mrs T: "I cut taxes because I thought we would get a giving society. And we haven't."'

The pace of change and the likelihood that much will alter in the future

If Mrs Thatcher did not think that much had changed, optimism abounds in the charitable and voluntary world that it is possible to increase significantly the numbers of people giving and the size of their gifts. The frequency of sector-supported efforts to promote generic giving – including the Giving Campaign (2001–04), the Philanthropy Review (2011) and the Give More campaign (2012–13) – is testament to this. By contrast, the previous section highlights stability rather than dramatic change in levels of giving.

Does this mean that, within broadly stable totals, it is impossible to achieve some degree of redistribution of charitable effort between causes or communities, or changes in the way individuals make decisions about how to allocate charitable funds?

We have used several environmental analogies in this book, including the suggestion in Chapter 5 that intermediaries 'warm up' the concept of 'cold charity'. The concept of 'charity deserts' (Chapter 3) is a resonant phrase but discussion of the topic generally fails to observe that deserts result from long-term climatic change. The locations where there are few registered charities were not 'deserted' as charitable organizations were always in short supply in those places. Historical investigations into the availability of voluntary resources show this consistently, whether we refer to endowments for free school places in the nineteenth century (Owen, 1964), hospital provision in the early twentieth century (Gorsky, et al., 1999; Mohan, 2003) or the funding of social services charities in interwar Britain (Jennings, 1945). So we should not expect substantial change in the short term in the distribution of charitable organizations.

But if we accept that the metaphor of a desert is useful for visualizing the geographic distribution of charities, how might these 'deserts' be irrigated? There are some efforts that are beginning to alter the charitable landscape at the margins, such as community foundations, which seek to pool resources over a large geographical area and thereby enable a more strategic and targeted approach to funding. To date, however, total funding from such foundations has been relatively small-scale (in 2013–14 the 48 community foundations across the UK distributed £65 million in grants[1]) and is variable between different community foundations and their funders (Jung et al., 2013).

Elsewhere, for example, in the USA, some 'place-based' initiatives have focused on the contribution of philanthropic initiatives within wider place-based programs of regeneration (Hopkins and Ferris, 2015). The criticism, which is not novel, is that these initiatives do not address causes of the decline of places, which are rooted in inequalities of income, wealth and political power (Dreier, 2015). That verdict could also be applied to the relatively small-scale post-2010 initiatives piloted recently in the UK, which have emphasized the formation of voluntary organizations, the granting of small amounts of money to community

DOI: 10.1057/9781137522658.0010

organizers or funding streams which are open to applications from areas that have not had many grants from particular funders.[2]

The scope for policies that allocate resources to disadvantaged areas is small given the public funding policies of the government elected in 2015. Other approaches favoured, such as the encouragement of business engagement with the voluntary sector, as in the Conservative Party's 2015 election pledge to grant paid leave to volunteer for employees in large organizations (Conservative Party, 2015, p. 45), are obviously subject to the limitation that areas with few private businesses also tend to be those with few charitable organizations.

The problem of an absence of charitable endeavour could of course be exacerbated as austerity bites (for initial studies of the process, not specifically focussed on charities, see Meegan et al., 2015; Milbourne, 2015). Many of the communities that have experienced – and which will in the future experience – substantial public funding reductions, are areas where there are relatively few registered charities. These are also locations that will face competition for voluntary resources (time and money) as new models for public service delivery are developed that involve greater co-production between local authorities and community groups.

Not only do such communities have fewer resources in organizational numbers, the voluntary organizations they have tend to be large, professionalized and heavily reliant on public funding. This is in contrast to the ecologies of charity we discovered in quantitative and qualitative work: in prosperous neighbourhoods we find strong numbers of organizations often working in fields that contribute to a high quality of life in those areas, with qualitative work showing that these are characterized by strong networks of volunteer-led organizations, which serve to recycle resources effectively within the community (Lindsey, 2013). Further, as discussed in Chapter 5, those charities with resources to invest in fundraising and communication functions are best placed to reap success in terms of generating voluntary income. A challenge for policy is therefore to match needs and resources in a more systematic way. This in turn directs attention to the public policy environment.

As to the pattern of allocation of charitable funds between causes, our discussion in Chapter 4 suggests that the processes underpinning donations by individuals are somewhat idiosyncratic and rely primarily on personal preferences. This in turn means that we cannot expect a

DOI: 10.1057/9781137522658.0010

great deal in terms of a systematic matching between donor preferences and either areas of disadvantage or previously under-resourced areas of activity, as Frumkin (2006, p. 153) notes:

> When the private values of the donor are a starting point, charitable giving takes on an expressive character that is quite distinct from the espoused needs and desires of the broad public. Reciprocity and the sense of giving something back does not necessarily lead to the most pressing public needs being selected for funding. Rather, it often leads straight into the personal life experiences and values of the donor.

Even those individual donors aspiring to make more objective philanthropic choices are faced with myriad charitable causes competing in a crowded marketplace, with limited time to assess the merits of the possible alternatives. Some guidance is available, for example, from 'charity ratings' websites and from resources produced by individuals and organizations aligned with the 'effective altruism' movement. But on the whole charitable choices continue to result from identification between donors and causes, including tastes, personal preferences and autobiographical connections.

Echoing attitudinal findings in Chapter 1, confidence in recipient organizations is important, as is a belief that giving ought to be enjoyable and enriching. Chapter 4 demonstrates that causes therefore tend to attract support by helping donors identify with their beneficiaries, providing reassurance they can have confidence in the recipient organization, and presenting donors with some type of personal enrichment as a result of that action.

The process of donation is not frictionless, and is mediated by philanthropic intermediaries (Chapter 5). Insights from our studies of the role of intermediaries are that fundraising is, at root, about building meaningful relationships with donors, in a donor-centred process which advocates a focus on the people making gifts, rather than the gifts they make, and an emphasis on the dual benefits for both parties in the transactions.

Current policy initiatives and debates

What kind of initiatives are being implemented, and might they have any effect on the situation described in this book? Individuals cannot be

DOI: 10.1057/9781137522658.0010

compelled to give to charity and, for the reasons explained in Chapters 2–5, dramatic sea changes seem unlikely.

Since 1990 the key policy lever in this regard has been tax reliefs for charitable donations, yet the rationale for reducing the price of giving for income tax payers is not clear, as Reich (2012) forcefully argues: whether it is a 'tax base rationale' acknowledging that tax payers have not themselves consumed the goods or services being paid for, or a 'subsidy rationale' seeking to achieve social benefits at a cheaper cost than the foregone tax revenue, or a 'pluralism rationale' hoping to foster a diverse, decentralized and civil society. Reich believes the latter rationale is most compelling, yet notes this is a cause-neutral argument because:

> 'The public good or social benefit being produced is civil society itself, not the catalogue of public goods or benefits produced by the roster of organizations that constitute civil society'. (p. 188)

So the jury remains out on the justification for charity tax reliefs, and whether they might aggravate, rather than mitigate, inequalities (Reich, 2006).

A principal initiative backed by the government of 2010–15 and the government elected in 2015 has been around the theme of 'nudging' people towards more pro-social behaviours (John et al., 2011), the institutional expression of which is the Behavioural Change Unit, created and funded by the government before becoming a social purpose company in 2014, known as the Behavioural Insights Team. In this case, nudging means trying to persuade people to give more to charity, stimulated by the receipt of information or prompts of some kind.

There has been evidence of successful 'nudges', such as prompting people to think about making a bequest when they are in the process of making a will (Behavioural Insights Team, 2014). Such initiatives are in the early stages, but our understanding of 'accumulated advantage' suggests that new techniques of fundraising will generate biggest returns for the organizations that are already large (see, e.g., Breeze et al., 2011).

Successive governments have also opened up public services to greater contestation and competition, arguing that this provides great opportunities for Third Sector organizations to compete in markets. This raises questions about how such markets operate and are regulated, including the view that it is difficult for charities to get a toehold in markets that are heavily dominated by big private companies. Thus far the experience of charitable organizations in these markets has not been very satisfactory,

DOI: 10.1057/9781137522658.0010

being squeezed out by large-scale commercial providers of services (Damm, 2014). Other new forms of funding involve greater marketization through the establishment of Social Impact Bonds (SIBs), whereby the social returns achieved by third sector organizations generate a payback (Breeze and Lloyd, 2013, pp. 57–58), but this raises questions regarding which organizations and where? And on what basis should we permit social investors to gain returns that ought to be socialized?

More generally, we question whether it is realistic to expect a substantial shift in the distribution of individual donations or charitable legacies between causes. One reason for this is the concentration of resources that already exists, such that new entrants are competing with very large, established organizations. Occasionally there are events that buck the trend such as major appeals in response to famine or disasters: around 80 per cent of the UK population responded to the Tsunami earthquake in December 2004 which raised a record-breaking high of £392 million (CAF, 2011), but such peaks in giving have not been accompanied by a sustained upward shift in levels of donations. And new charitable organizations can take root and flourish, for example, the military charity Help for Heroes was founded in 2007 and in under a decade has become one of the UK's largest charities, as a result of mobilizing considerable media support and fundraising.

But given the evidence in Chapters 4 and 5 about the ways in which donors are motivated to support causes as a result of processes of identification, personal preferences and biographical drivers, it seems difficult to envisage circumstances in which substantial additional funds could be generated for less 'popular' causes such as organizations supporting former addicts or prisoners, to say nothing of the need to raise funds to sustain basic public services. Our attitudinal surveys (Chapter 1) suggest that even while people may have reservations about the competence and efficiency of charities, they still have quite definite ideas about where the boundary between responsibility for funding the provision of various services ought to be drawn – though they might also give their time to support public services in their communities.

The public also questions the proliferation of charities, and concerns about duplication and proliferation – the converse of the concentration of resources described in Chapter 2 – are regularly vented. However, excessive regulation of this seems unlikely, since it would work against the logic of charity, which involves the freedom to experiment and innovate, however idiosyncratic the cause might appear. Charities will still have

DOI: 10.1057/9781137522658.0010

to work to command the confidence of the public, particularly in the wake of controversies in 2015 about fundraising tactics, notably via the telephone and direct mail, with the charity sector finding itself accused of operating in a uniquely 'aggressive' and unacceptable manner, leading to calls for new and stricter regulation (Etherington, 2015). Such complaints are not entirely new. A respondent to the Mass Observation inquiry in the 1940s – an 80-year-old working-class male from Tottenham – railed against his address details being shared with charities , as a result of which he was deluged with requests for support, to which he responded in an ad hoc way – although he blamed the Post Office rather than fund-raisers for revealing his address (Mass Observation, 1947, p. 11).

And charities will still have to contend with the lack of political understanding of, and appreciation for, the diverse roles they play in building a pluralistic civil society – sometimes acting in ways that align with political priorities, sometimes acting in ways that challenge political power, and often acting in ways that have little or no bearing on political activity either way.

As we finish writing this book in September 2015, speakers at the political party conferences made comments that echo many of our themes, saying that politicians have an 'instrumentalist view of the charity sector', 'seem to treat charities as a means to an end' and 'use charities for photo opportunities but then ignore them',[3] but also arguing that charities 'have become more political in the way they campaign' and need to be clearer with donors about where their money is being spent.[4] This suggests that charities have an uphill struggle to educate politicians about the distinctiveness of their role and contribution to society, which includes campaigning and political activity in support of their charitable objectives. Charities also need to respond and make changes, particu-larly in regard to fundraising practices, if they wish to sustain – and regain – the public trust and confidence that is so crucial for securing private support.

The message of this book, though, is ultimately a different one: that for the most part, private giving occurs without reference to any govern-mental agenda, and cannot be easily 'turned up' or redirected by policy levers. Supporters of charity will take heart from the historian Frank Prochaska (2014), who pointed to the continued vitality of charities with the resonant phrase 'we are always with the poor'. Maybe we can rephrase this in the light of the present reality. Charity is always with us, but not always in the places and causes where it is most needed. The

DOI: 10.1057/9781137522658.0010

logic of charity cannot result in a proportionate matching of needs and resources, regardless of the hopes of politicians. And that situation is not likely to change, given the inherently individualistic nature of the processes whereby individuals give financial support to charities.

Notes

1 According to the website of the umbrella organization UK Community Foundations, http://ukcommunityfoundations.org (viewed 2 October 2015)
2 For example, the Big Local Trust – http://localtrust.org.uk – and the community organizers programme – https://www.gov.uk/government/news/government-names-new-partner-to-deliver-community-organisers
3 http://www.civilsociety.co.uk/governance/news/content/20473/politicians_often_value_charities_only_as_a_means_to_an_end_labour_conference_hears?utm_source=29September+2015+Fundraising&utm_campaign=29+Sept+2015+Fundraising&utm_medium=email and http://www.civilsociety.co.uk/governance/news/content/20492/mps_want_to_be_on_a_charitys_side_only_when_it_suits_them_labour_conference_hears?utm_source=1+October+2015+Fundraising&utm_campaign=1+Oct+2015+Fundraising&utm_medium=email
4 http://www.civilsociety.co.uk/governance/news/content/20517/conservative_mp_some_charities_have_become_more_political_in_the_way_they_campaign?utm_source=5+October+2015+Fundraising&utm_campaign=5+October+2015%3A+Fundraising&utm_medium=email

DOI: 10.1057/9781137522658.0010

Bibliography

Andreoni, J. (1990) Impure altruism and donations
to public goods: a theory of warm glow giving. *The
Economic Journal*, 100, 401, 464–77.

Andreoni, J. (1993) An experimental test of the public-
goods crowding out hypothesis. *American Economic
Review*, 83, 1317–27.

Atkinson, A. (2013) Wealth and inheritance in britain
from 1896 to the present, London: Centre for the
Analysis of Social Exclusion (CASE), paper 178.
Available at http://sticerd.lse.ac.uk/dps/case/cp/
casepaper178.pdf

Atkinson, A., Backus, P. G., Micklewright, J., Pharoah, C.
and Schnepf, S. V. (2012) Charitable giving for overseas
development: UK trends over a quarter century. *Journal
of the Royal Statistical Society: Series A (Statistics in
Society)*, 175, 167–90.

Backus, P. and Clifford, D. (2013) Are big charities
becoming more dominant? Cross-sectional and
longitudinal perspectives. *Journal of Royal Statistical
Society: Series A*, 176, 761–76.

Backus, P. and Mohan, J. (forthcoming) Charitable causes
in twentieth-century England: a quantitative analysis of
'foundation' dates. *Voluntas*, forthcoming.

Baker, L., Harris, M. Moran, R. and Morgan, G. (2012) *The
Impact of the Public Benefit Requirement in the Charities
Act 2006: Perceptions, Knowledge and Experience.*
Institute for Voluntary Action Research and Sheffield
Hallam University.

Ball, S. (2008) New philanthropy, new networks and new governance in education. *Political Studies*, 56, 747–65.

Barnett, S. and Saxon-Harrold, S. (1992) Interim report: charitable giving, in R. Jowell, G. Brook, Taylor R. Prior (eds.), *British Social Attitudes: The 9th Report*, pp. 195–208.

Bauman, Z. (2000) *The Individualized Society*. Cambridge: Polity Press.

Beck, U. and Beck-Gernsheim, E. (2001) *Individualization: Institutionalized Individualism and its Social and Political Consequences*. London: Sage.

Behavioural Insights Team (2014) *Applying Behavioural Insights to Charitable Giving*. London: Cabinet Office.

Bekkers, R. (2005) It's not all in the ask. effects and effectiveness of recruitment. Paper presented at 34rd Annual ARNOVA Conference, Washington, DC, USA.

Bell, J. and Cornelius, M. (2014) *Underdeveloped: A National Study of Challenges Facing Nonprofit Fundraising*. CompassPoint and the Evelyn and Walter Haas Jr. Fund.

Ben-Ner, A. (1986) Non-profit Organisations: why do they exist in market economies? in S. Rose-Ackerman (ed.), *The Economics of Nonprofit Institutions: Studies in Structure and Policy*. Oxford: Oxford University Press.

Berridge, V. and Mold, A. (2010) *Voluntary Action and Illegal Drugs*. Basingstoke: Palgrave Macmillan.

Beveridge, W. (1948) *Voluntary Action: A Report on Methods of Social Advance*. London: Allen and Unwin.

Billis, D. (2010) *Hybrid Organizations and the Third Sector: Challenges for Practice, Theory and Policy*. Basingstoke: Palgrave Macmillan.

Billis, D. and Glennerster, H. (1998) Human services and the voluntary sector: towards a theory of comparative advantage. *Journal of Social Policy*, 27, 79–98.

Bloland, H. G. (2002) No longer emerging, fundraising is a profession. *CASE International Journal of Education Advancement*, 3, 1, 7–21.

Body, A. and Breeze, B. (2015) *Rising to the Challenge: A Study of Philanthropic Support for 'Unpopular' Causes*. Canterbury: Centre for Philanthropy, University of Kent.

Bourdieu, P. (1998) *Practical Reason: On the Theory of Action*, English translation, first published in French in 1994. Oxford: Blackwell.

Braithwaite, C. (1938) *The Voluntary Citizen: An Enquiry into the Place of Philanthropy in the Community*. London: Methuen.

DOI: 10.1057/9781137522658.0011

Breeze, B. (2012) *Coutts Million Pound Donor Report 2012*. London: Coutts & Co.

Breeze, B. (2013) 'How Donors Choose Charities'. *Voluntary Sector Review*, 4, 2.

Breeze, B. (ed.) (2014) *Great British Philanthropy: Growing a Fellowship of Donors to Support Local Communities*. London: UK Community Foundations.

Breeze, B. (forthcoming) *The New Fundraisers*. Bristol: Policy Press.

Breeze, B. and Lloyd, T. (2013) *Richer Lives: Why Rich People Give*. London: Directory of Social Change.

Breeze, B., Halfpenny, P., and Wilding, K. (2015). Giving in the United Kingdom: Philanthropy embedded in a Welfare State Society. In P. Wiepking & F. Handy (eds.) *The Palgrave Handbook of Global Philanthropy*. Basingstoke: Palgrave.

Breeze, B. and Scaife, W. (2015) Encouraging generosity: the practice and organzation of fund-raising across nations, in P. Wiepking and F. Handy (eds.), *The Palgrave Handbook of Global Philanthropy*. Basingstoke: Palgrave.

Breeze, B., Wilkinson, I. M., Gouwenberg, B. and Schuyt, T. (2011) *Giving in Evidence: Fundraising from Philanthropy in European Universities*. European Commission.

Brenton, M. (1985) *The Voluntary Sector in British Social Services*. London: Longman.

Brest, P. (2012) A decade of outcome-oriented philanthropy. *Stanford Social Innovation Review*, Spring 2012.

Brest, P. and Harvey, H. (2008) *Money Well Spent: A Strategic Plan for Smart Philanthropy*. New York: Bloomberg Press.

Brookes, M. (2010) Is Saving a Donkey Morally Wrong? NPC blog, http://www.thinknpc.org/blog/is-saving-a-donkey-morally-wrong/

Bryant, W. K., Slaughter, H. J., Kang, H. and Tax, A. (2003) Participating in philanthropic activities: donating money and time. *Journal of Consumer Policy*, 26, 43–73.

Burk, P. (2003) *Donor Centered Fundraising*. Chicago, IL: Burk & Associates Ltd.

Burlingame, D. (1993) Altruism and philanthropy: definitional issues. *Essays on Philanthopy, No. 10*. Bloomington, IN: Indiana University Press.

Burne James, S. (2015) Sector condemns Eric Pickles comments on sock-puppet charities, *Third Sector*, 3 March 2015. Available online

DOI: 10.1057/9781137522658.0011

at http://www.thirdsector.co.uk/sector-condemns-eric-pickles-comments-sock-puppet-charities/policy-and-politics/article/1336505

Burnett, K. (2002, 2nd edition) *Relationship Fundraising: A Donor-Based Approach to the Business of Raising Money.* Oxford: John Wiley & Sons.

Cabinet Office (2011) *Giving White Paper.* Cm. 8084. London: HMSO.

CAF (2011) *Disaster Monitor 2011.* Available online at https://www.cafonline. org/about-us/publications/2011-publications/caf-disaster-monitor-2011

CAF (2014) *UK Giving 2013.* London: Charities Aid Foundation.

CAF (2015) *UK Giving 2014.* London: Charities Aid Foundation.

Centre for Social Justice (2013) *Something's Got to Give: The State of Britain's Voluntary and Community Sector.* London: Centre for Social Justice.

Centre for Social Justice (2014) *Social Solutions: Enabling Grassroots Charities to Tackle Poverty.* London: Centre for Social Justice.

Clifford D. (2012) Voluntary sector organisations working at the neighbourhood level in England: patterns by local area deprivation. *Environment and Planning A*, 44, 1148–64.

Clifford, D., Geyne Rajme, F. and Mohan, J. (2013) Variations between organisations and localities in government funding of third sector activity: Evidence from the National Survey of Third Sector Organisations in England. *Urban Studies*, 50, 959–76.

Clifford, D. and Mohan, J. (forthcoming) The sources of income of English and Welsh charities: an organisation-level perspective, *Voluntas.* Pre-publication version available at http://link.springer. com/article/10.1007%2Fs11266-015-9628-5

Clotfelter, C. T. (ed.) (1992) *Who Benefits from the Nonprofit Sector?* Chicago, IL: Chicago University Press.

Connolly, P. (2011) The best of the humanistic and technocratic: why the most effective work in philanthropy requires a balance. *The Foundation Review*, 3, 1 and 2.

Conservative Party (2007) *A Stronger Society: Voluntary Action in the 21st Century*, www.Conservatives.com/~/media/files/green%20papers/voluntary_green_paper.ashx?dl==true.

Conservative Party (2015) *The Conservative Party Election Manifesto 2015.* Available at https://www.conservatives.com/manifesto

Csikszentmihalyi, M. (2006) Concluding thoughts, in W. Damon and S. Verducci (eds.), *Taking Philanthropy Seriously: Beyond Noble Intentions to Responsible Giving.* Bloomington: Indiana University Press.

DOI: 10.1057/9781137522658.0011

Cunningham, H. (2015) *A History of Western Philanthropy*. London: Centre for Giving and Philanthropy.

Daly, S. (2011) Philanthropy, the Big Society and emerging philanthropic relationships in the UK. *Public Management Review*, 13, 8, 1077–94.

Damm, C. (2014) A mid-term review of third sector involvement in the Work Programme. *Voluntary Sector Review*, 5, 1, 97–116.

Deakin, N. (2001) *In Search of Civil Society*. London: Routledge.

D'Eustachio, R. (2015) Funlanthropy. In *Giving Magazine*, launch edition.

Derrida, J. (1992) *Given Time: 1. Counterfeit Money.* Chicago and London: University of Chicago Press.

Dobkin Hall, P. (2013) Philanthropy, the nonprofit sector and the democratic dilemma. *Daedalus*, 142, 139–58.

Dreier, P. (2015) Rich ghettos/poor ghettos, in E. Hopkins and J. Ferris (eds.), *Place-Based Initiatives in the Context of Public Policy and Markets*. Los Angeles: University of Southern California Sol Price Institute for Public Policy, pp. 45–46.

Duncan, B. (2004) A theory of impact philanthropy. *Journal of Public Economics*, 88, 2159–80.

Duncan Smith, I. (2005) *Big charities are becoming an arm of big government, warns former Conservative leader*, Speech to 'Britain's most admired charities' awards ceremony, 3 November 2005. Available online at http://www.centreforsocialjustice.org.uk/UserStorage/pdf/Press%20releases%202010%20-/pressSpeechIDS02.pdf

Eikenberry, A. (2009) *Giving Circles: Philanthropy, Voluntary Association, and Democracy.* Bloomington: Indiana University Press.

Eikenberry, A. and Breeze, B. (2015) Growing philanthropy through collaboration: the landscape of giving circles in the United Kingdom and Ireland. *Voluntary Sector Review*, 6, 1.

Eikenberry, A., Brown, M. and Lukins, L. (2015) *A Study of the Impact of Participation in UK Giving Circles*. https://drive.google.com/file/d/0B_aU_r-0ntPWOWxpT3QwS0RVc3c/view

Etherington, S. (2015) *Regulating Fundraising for the Future: Trust in Charities, Confidence in Fundraising Regulation*. London: NCVO.

Farnsworth, K. (2015) *The British Corporate Welfare State: Public Provision for Private Businesses*. Sheffield: Sheffield Political Economic Resaarch Institute, SPERI paper 24. Available at http://speri.dept.shef.ac.uk/2015/07/08/speri-paper-british-corporate-welfare-state/

DOI: 10.1057/9781137522658.0011

Fenton, N., P. Golding, et al. (1993) *Charities, Media and Public Opinion*. Department of Social Sciences, University of Loughborough.

Field, F. (2015) *To Him That Hath Shall Be Given: A Call to Arms*. Lecture to the Charity Commission, September 2015. Available at https://www.gov.uk/government/uploads/system/uploads/attachment_data/file/461674/frankfield160915.pdf

Fleishman, J. (2007) *The Foundation: A Great American Secret*. New York: Public Affairs.

Frumkin, P. (2006) *Strategic Giving: The Art and Science of Philanthropy*. Chicago and London: University of Chicago Press.

Fyfe, N. and Milligan, C. (2003b) Space, citizenship and voluntarism: critical reflections on the voluntary welfare sector in Glasgow. *Environment and Planning A*, 35, 2069–86.

Fyfe, N. and Milligan, C. (2004) Putting the voluntary sector in its place: geographical perspectives on voluntary activity and social welfare in Glasgow. *Journal of Social Policy*, 33, 73–93.

Glennie, A. and Whillans-Welldrake, A.-G. (2014) *Charity Street: The Value of Charity to British Households*. London: IPPR.

Goldberg, S. H. (2009) *Billions of Drops in Millions of Buckets: Why Philanthropy Doesn't Advance Social Progress*. Hoboken, NJ: John Wiley and Sons.

Gorsky, M., Mohan, J. and Powell, M. (1999) British voluntary hospitals 1871–1938: the geography of provision and utilisation. *Journal of Historical Geography*, 25, 4, 463–82.

Gorsky, M., Mohan, J. and Powell, M. (2002) The financial health of voluntary hospitals in inter-war Britain. *Economic History Review*, LV, 533–57.

Gorsky, M., Mohan, J., with Willis, T. (2006) *Mutualism and Health Care, British Hospital Contributory Schemes in the 20th Century*. Manchester: Manchester University Press.

Green, D. (1993) *Reinventing Civil Society: The Rediscovery of Welfare without Politics*. London: Institute of Economic Affairs.

Hansmann, H. B. (1980) The role of nonprofit enterprise. *The Yale Law Journal*, 89, 835–901.

Harris, R. and Seldon, A. (1979) *Overruled on Welfare*. London: Institute of Economic Affairs.

Hatch, S. (1980) *Outside the State: Voluntary Organisations in Three English Towns*. London: Croom Helm.

von Hayek, F. (1944) *The Road to Serfdom*. London: Routledge

DOI: 10.1057/9781137522658.0011

HM Government (2011) *Open Public Services White Paper*. Cm. 8145. London: HMSO.

HM Revenue and Customs (HMRC) (2015) *UK charity tax relief statistics, 1990–91 to 2014–15*. London: HMRC. Available online at https://www.gov.uk/government/uploads/system/uploads/ attachment_data/file/456405/CommentaryDocument.pdf.

Hopkins, E. and Ferris, J. (eds.) (2015) *Place-Based Initiatives in the Context of Public Policy and Markets*. Los Angeles: University of Southern California Sol Price Institute for Public Policy.

Horn, L. and Gardner, H. (2006) The lonely profession, in W. Damon and S. Verducci (eds.), *Taking Philanthropy Seriously: Beyond Noble Intentions to Responsible Giving*. Bloomington: Indiana University Press.

Institute for Philanthropy (2010) *The Power of Now: Spend Out Trusts and Foundations in the UK*. London: Institute for Philanthropy.

Ipsos MORI (2008) *National Survey of Third Sector Organisations: Analytical Report*. London: Cabinet Office.

James, E. (1983) How nonprofits grow: a model. *Journal of Policy Analysis and Management*, 2, 350–66.

Jencks, C. (1987) Who gives to what? in W. Powell (ed.), *The NonProfit Sector: A Research Handbook*. New Haven: Yale University Press.

Jennings, H. (1945) Voluntary social services in urban areas, in H. Mess (ed.), *Voluntary Social Services since 1918*. London: Kegan Paul, pp. 28–39.

John, P., et al. (2011) *Nudge, Nudge, Think, Think: Using Experiments to Change Civic Behaviour*. London: Bloomsbury.

Jones, G., Meegan, R., Kennett, P. and Croft, J. (2015) The uneven impact of austerity on the voluntary and community sector: a tale of two cities. *Urban Studies*, forthcoming. Available at http://usj.sagepub. com/content/early/2015/05/22/0042098015587240.abstract.

Jung, T., Harrow, J. and Phillips, S. (2013) Developing a better understanding of community foundations in the UK's localisms. *Policy and Politics*, 41, 409–27.

Kane, D. and Clark, J. (2009) The regional distribution of charity expenditure. Paper presented at the Researching the Voluntary Sector Conference, September 2009.

Kane, D., Clark, J., Clifford, D., Mohan, J., Dobbs, J. and Bass, P. (2013) Collecting and classifying data from charity accounts for England and Wales. *Third Sector Research Centre Working Paper*, 93.

DOI: 10.1057/9781137522658.0011

Kendall, J. and Knapp, M. (1996) *The Voluntary Sector in the United Kingdom*. Manchester: Manchester University Press.

Knight, B. (1993) *Voluntary Action*. London: Centris.

Komter, A. (2005) *Social Solidarity and the Gift*. Cambridge: Cambridge University Press.

Krakovsky, M. (2015) *The Middleman Economy: How Brokers, Agents, Dealers, and Everyday Matchmakers Create Value and Profit*. New York: Palgrave Macmillan.

Kramer, R. (1990) Change and continuity in British voluntary organisations, 1976–1988, *Voluntas*, 1, 33–60.

Leonhardt, D. (2008) What makes people give? *New York Times*, 9 March 2008.

Leslie, Brian, Noonan, K. and Nohavec, C. (2015) Understanding philanthropy consulting: a tool to identify the roles and capabilities needed from external support. *The Foundation Review*, 7, 1, article 5.

Lewis, J. (1993) Developing the mixed economy of care: emerging issues for voluntary organisations. *Journal of Social Policy*, 22, 173–92.

Lillya, D., Reynolds, J. and Zagnojute, G. (2015) *The Guide to UK Company Giving* 2015/15. London: Directory of Social Change.

Lincoln, S. and Saxton, J. (2012) *Major Donor Giving Research Report: A Synthesis of the Current Research into Major Donors and Philanthropic Giving*. London: nfpSynergy/Institute of Fundraising.

Lindsey, R. (2013) Exploring local hotspots and deserts: investigating the local distribution of charitable resources. *Voluntary Sector Review*, 4, 95–116.

Lindsey, R., Mohan, J. et al. (forthcoming) *Continuity and Change in Voluntary Action*. Bristol: Policy Press.

Lindstrom, J. and Henson, S. (2011) *What Does the Public Think, Know and Do about Aid and Development?* Brighton: Institute of Development Studies.

Mackenzie, S. (ed.) (2008, 3rd edition) *A Guide to Giving*. London: Association of Charitable Foundations.

Mass Observation (1947) *Voluntary Social Service Inquiry, Report No. 2: Aspects of Charity* (file report 2508). Brighton: Mass Observation.

May, T. (1997) *Social Research: Issues, Methods and Processes*. Buckingham: Open University Press.

Milbourne, L. (2013) *Voluntary Sector in Transition: Hard Times or New Opportunities?* Bristol: Policy Press.

DOI: 10.1057/9781137522658.0011

Milbourne, L. and Cushman, M. (2014) Complying, transforming or resisting in the new austerity: realigning social welfare and independent action among English voluntary organisations. *Journal of Social Policy*, 44, 463–85.

Mill, J. S. (1848) *Principles of Political Economy*. Available online at http://www.econlib.org/library/Mill/mlP73.html#d121.

Mohan, J. (2003) Voluntarism, municipalism and welfare: the geography of hospital utilization in England in the 1930s. *Transactions, Institute of British Geographers*, 28, 1, 55–74.

Mohan, J. (2012) Entering the lists: what can we learn from the voluntary sector in England from listings produced by local infrastructure bodies? *Voluntary Sector Review*, 3, 2, 197–215.

Mohan, J. (2015) Charity deserts and social justice: exploring variations in the distribution of charitable organisations and their resources in England, in B. Morvaridi (ed.), *New Philanthropy and Social Justice*. Bristol: Policy Press, pp. 191–212.

Mohan, J., Clark, J., Kane, D. and Wilding, K. (2011) *Trends in the North: what we have learned from the quantitative programme of the Third Sector Trends study*. Available at www.nr-foundation.org.uk/resources/third-sector-trends-study

Mohan, J. and Gorsky, M. (2001) *Don't Look Back? Voluntary and Charitable Finance of Hospital Care in Britain, Past and Present*. London: Office of Health Economics.

Mohan, J. and McKay, S. (forthcoming) *Highly-Paid Staff in English and Welsh Charities: Worth the Money?* Submitted for publication.

Mohan, J. and Wilding, K. (2009) Economic Downturns and the Voluntary Sector: What can we learn from historical evidence? *History and Policy*, policy paper 85. Available at www.historyandpolicy.org/archive/policy-paper-85.html

Morgan, G. G. (2010) The use of charitable status as a basis for regulation of nonprofit accounting. *Voluntary Sector Review*, 1, 209–32.

Morgan, G. G. (2011) The use of UK charity accounts data for researching the performance of voluntary organisations. *Voluntary Sector Review*, 2, 213–30.

Morgan, G. G. (2012) Public benefit and charitable status: assessing a 20 year process of reforming the primary legal framework for voluntary activity in the UK. *Voluntary Sector Review*, 3, 1, 69–93.

Morris, D. (2012) Charities and the Big Society: a doomed coalition? *Legal Studies*, 32, 132–53.

DOI: 10.1057/9781137522658.0011

Mullin, R. (2007) Two thousand years of disreputable history, in J. Mordaunt and R. Paton (eds.), *Thoughtful Fundraising: Concepts, Issues and Perspectives*. Abingdon, Oxon: Routledge.

National Council for Voluntary Organisations (NCVO) (2015) *The UK Civil Society Almanac 2015*. London: NCVO

Odendahl, T. J. (1989) Charitable giving patterns by elites in the United States, in V. Hodgkinson and R. W. Lyman (eds.), *The Future of the Nonprofit Sector: Challenges, Changes and Policy Considerations*. San Francisco: Jossey-Bass.

Odendahl, T. (1990) *Charity Begins at Home: Generosity and Self-Interest among the Philanthropic Elite*. New York: Basic Books.

Ortmann, A. (1996) Review of 'Who benefits from the nonprofit sector?' by Charles T Clotfelter. *Nonprofit and Voluntary Sector Quarterly*, 25, 2, 248–58.

Osteen, M. (ed.) (2002) *The Question of the Gift: Essays across Disciplines*. London and New York: Routledge.

Ostrander, S. (2007) The growth of donor control: revisiting the social relations of philanthropy. *Nonprofit and Voluntary Sector Quarterly*, 36, 2, 356–72.

Ostrower, F. (1995) *Why the Wealthy Give: The Culture of Elite Philanthropy*. Princeton, NJ: Princeton University Press.

Owen, D. (1964) *English Philanthropy, 1660–1960*. Boston: Harvard University Press.

Panas, J. (1984) *Mega Gifts: Who Gives Them, Who Gets Them?* Chicago: Bonus Books Inc.

Payton, R. L. and Moody, M. P. (2008) *Understanding Philanthropy: Its Meaning and Mission*. Bloomington: Indiana University Press.

Pharoah, C., Jenkins, R. and Goddard, K. (2015) *Foundation Giving Trends 2015*, London: Association of Charitable Foundations. Available online at http://www.acf.org.uk/uploadedFiles/ Publications_and_resources/Giving%20Trends%20Top%20300%20 Foundation%20Grant-Makers%202015.pdf

Prochaska, F. (1990) Philanthropy, in F. M. L. Thompson (ed.), *The Cambridge Social History of Britain 1750–1950*. Cambridge: Cambridge University Press.

Prochaska, F. (2014) *The state of charity*. Lecture to the Charity Commission, September 2014. Available at https://www.gov.uk/ government/uploads/system/uploads/attachment_data/file/356191/ Lecture_-_Dr_Frank_Prochaska.pdf

Reich, R. (2005) A Failure of Philanthropy. *Stanford Social Innovation Review*, Winter.

Reich, R. (2006) Philanthropy and its uneasy relation to equality, in W. Damon and S. Verducci (eds.), *Taking Philanthropy Seriously: Beyond Noble Intentions to Responsible Giving*. Indianapolis: Indiana University Press.

Reich, R. (2012) Political theory of philanthropy, in P. Illingworth, T. Pogge, and L. Wenar (eds.), *Giving Well: The Ethics of Philanthropy*. Oxford: Oxford University Press.

Robson, C. (1993) *Real World Research: A Resource for Social Scientists and Practitioner-researchers*. Oxford: Blackwell.

Rosenthal, J. (1972) *The Purchase of Paradise: Gift Giving and the Aristocracy 1307–1485*. London: Routledge and Kegan Paul.

Royal College of Psychiatrists (2009) *Mental Health and the Economic Downturn*. London: Royal College of Psychiatrists.

Salamon, L. (1987) Partners in public service: the scope and theory of government-non-profit relations, in W. W. Powell (ed.), *The Non-profit Sector: A Research Handbook*. Newhaven, CT: Yale University Press.

Salamon, L. and Anheier, H. (1996) *The international classification of nonprofit organizations: ICNPO-Revision 1, 1996*. Working Papers of the Johns Hopkins Comparative Nonprofit Sector Project, no. 19. Baltimore, MD: The Johns Hopkins Institue for Policy Studies.

Salamon, L. and Anheier, H. (1997) *Defining the Nonprofit Sector*. Manchester: Manchester University Press.

Sargeant, A. and Jay, E. (2014, 3rd edition) *Fundraising Management: Analysis, Planning and Practice*. London: Routledge.

Sargeant, A. and Shang, J. (2011) *Growing Philanthropy in the United Kingdom*. Bristol: University of the West of England.

Sayer, A. (2015) *Why We Can't Afford the Rich*. Bristol: Policy Press.

Schambra, W. (2014) The coming showdown between philanthrolocalism and effective altruism. *Philanthropy Daily* blogpost 22/5/14 http://www.philanthropydaily.com/the-coming-showdown-between-philanthrolocalism-and-effective-altruism/

Scharf, K., Payne, A. and Smith, S. (2015) Online Fundraising. The Perfect Ask? *CAGE Discussion Paper* No. 194.

Schervish, P. G. and Havens, J. J. (1997) Social participation and charitable giving: a multivariate analysis. *Voluntas*, 8, 3, 235–60.

DOI: 10.1057/9781137522658.0011

Scott, R. W. (1995) *Institutions and Organizations*. Thousand Oaks, CA: Sage.

Seddon, N. (2007) *Who Cares? How State Funding and Political Activism Change Charity*. London: Civitas.

Seldon, A. (1990) *Capitalism*. Oxford: Blackwell.

Shawcross, W. (2012) Speech to the Association of Chief Executives of Voluntary Organisations (ACEVO), 1 November 2012. Available online at https://www.gov.uk/government/speeches/acevo-annual-conference-2012-william-shawcrosss-speech

Silber, I. (1998) Modern philanthropy: reassessing the viability of a maussian perspective, in W. James and N. J. Allen (eds.), *Marcell Mauss: A Centenary Tribute*. Oxford, New York: Berghahn.

Silber, I. (2012) The angry gift: A neglected facet of philanthropy. *Current Sociology*, 60, 3.

Singer, P. (2015) *The Most Good You Can Do: How Effective Altruism is Changing Ideas about Living Ethically*. New Haven: Yale University Press.

Smith, S. (2012) *Mind the gap: the growing generational divide in charitable giving: a research paper*. Tunbridge Wells: Charities Aid Foundation. Available at www.cafonline.org/pdf/1190H_PartyConf_MindTheGap.pdf

Smith, S., Cowley, E., McKenzie, T. and Pharoah, C. (2011) *Three Decades of Household Giving to Charity, 1978–2008*. Available at www.bristol.ac.uk/cmpo/publications/bulletin/summer11/smithcowley.pdf

Smith, C. and Davidson, H. (2014) *The Paradox of Generosity: Giving We Receive, Grasping We Lose*. Oxford University Press.

Snowdon, C. (2014) *The Sock Doctrine: What Can be Done about State-Funded Political Activism?* IEA discussion paper, 53. London: Institute of Economic Affairs.

Sokolowski, W. (1996) Show me the way to the next worthy deed: towards a microstructural theory of volunteering and giving. *Voluntas*, 7, 3, 259–78.

Stead, B. A. (1985) Corporate giving: a look at the arts. *Journal of Business Ethics*, 4, 3, 215–22.

Tierney, T. and Fleishman, J. (2011) *Give Smart: Philanthropy That Gets Results*. New York: Public Affairs Books.

Titmuss, R. (1970) *The Gift Relationship: From Human Blood to Social Policy*. London: George Allen & Unwin.

DOI: 10.1057/9781137522658.0011

UK Government (2010) *Every business commits*. Available at https://
www.gov.uk/government/uploads/system/uploads/attachment_data/
file/31972/11–859-every-business-commits.pdf

Wagner, D. (2000) *What's Love Got to Do With It?* New York:, The New
York Press.

Ware, A. (2012) The big society and Conservative politics: back to the
future or forward to the past? *Political Quarterly*, Supplement S1,
82–97.

Weisbrod, B. A. (1988) *The Nonprofit Economy*. Cambridge, MA: Harvard
University Press.

Wolch, J. and Geiger, R. (1983) The distribution of voluntary resources:
an exploratory analysis. *Environment and Planning A*, 15, 1067–82.

Wolfenden Committee (1978) *The future of voluntary organizations:
report of the Wolfenden Committee*. London: Croom Helm.

Wolpert, J. (1988) The geography of generosity: metropolitan disparities
in donations and support for amenities. *Annals of the Association of
American Geographers*, 78, 665–79.

Wolpert, J. (1996) *What Charity Can and Cannot Do*. New York: The
Twentieth Century Fund Press.

Zunz, O. (2011) *Philanthropy in America: A History*. Princeton: Princeton
University Press.

DOI: 10.1057/9781137522658.0011

Index

DOI: 10.1057/9781137522658.0012

DOI: 10.1057/9781137522658.0012

DOI: 10.1057/9781137522658.0012

DOI: 10.1057/9781137522658.0012